Gospel Meeting Sermons

by Johnie Edwards

ONESTONE
BIBLICAL RESOURCES

Published by:
One Stone Press
979 Lovers Lane
Bowling Green, KY 42103

Printed in the United States of America

ISBN-10: 1-941422-00-4
ISBN-13: 978-1-941422-00-7

ONE STONE
BIBLICAL RESOURCES

www.onestone.com

Foreword

I know of no greater need than sermon material for gospel meetings. I do not know of any man better qualified to publish this type of material than Johnie Edwards.

I have been acquainted with him for years. He has conducted many meetings. Large crowds attend, and many have obeyed the gospel as a result of his influence. Johnie's sermons are plain and yet full of material. I am sure this book will be a profit to many preachers.

After reading his material, you will see why he is in such demand for meeting work.

Robert Jackson
Nashville, Tennessee

Preface

Gospel Meeting Sermons is offered in the sincere hope that those young men who desire to preach the gospel of Jesus Christ can use these sermon outlines as a means to provoke their listeners to a more detailed study of the Word of God.

These gospel sermons have been preached in gospel meetings with much success in many parts of this country. They are simple, logically organized and abundantly supplied with book, chapter and verse to support each point. I pray that you will find these sermon outlines useful in your efforts to offer the simple gospel to those for whom you speak.

Johnie Edwards
October 1978

Contents

~ 1 ~

First of All

1 Corinthians 15:3-4

Introduction

I.   Paul introduces the phrase "first of all" to the Corinthians in I Corinthians 15:3-4.

II. There are many lessons that we need to learn by keeping things in the proper order. There are some things that must be put first.

Discussion

I.   First gave self to the Lord

   A. 2 Corinthians 8:5

      1. These Corinthians had gone beyond their ability. They exceeded that which Paul had hoped for them, for they were poor.

      2. They realized the greatest value they could give was to give self.

   B. 1 Timothy 4:16

   C. Other things will come easier if we will first of all give ourselves to the Lord.

II. If there be first a willing mind

   A. 2 Corinthians 8:12

B. God has always required that his people have a willing mind.

    1. Exodus 35:5

    2. 1 Chronicles 28:9

C. Things get done when we have a mind to work.

    1. Nehemiah 4:6

    2. This we need today.

III. Cleanse first the inside.

A. Matthew 23:26

B. Discuss context of Matthew 23:26.

C. Matthew 15:18-19

    1. The heart is important.

    2. The heart is the soul of what we do.

IV. First cast out the beam out of thine own eye.

A. Matthew 7:5

B. Beam is large and a mote is small.

C. Many see everybody's faults but their own!

    1. We need to keep ourselves clean so we can help others.

    2. 1 Timothy 5:22

V. First be reconciled to thy brother.

A. Matthew 5:23-24

B. God will not accept our worship when we are at odds with our brother.

    1. There is no need for us to try to worship God when we have aught against our brother.

    2. We must do all that we can to resolve these difficulties.

VI. He first findeth his own brother.

    A. John 1:40-42

    B. Andrew learned of Jesus, then first found and brought his brother to the Lord.

    C. The growth of the church depends a great deal on personal evangelism.

VII. Seek ye first the kingdom of God.

    A. Matthew 6:33

    B. Study the context of Matthew 6:25-34.

    C. One of the greatest needs of the church is to put the church and God's righteousness first.

    D. Putting the church first will cause:

        1. Every member to attend every service (Hebrews 10:25)

        2. The church to grow (1 Timothy 4:16)

        3. The material things to be added to us (Matthew 6:33)

Conclusion

I. If we expect to please God we must put first things first.

II. Why not give yourself to the Lord by obeying the gospel as we stand and sing?

~ 2 ~
Making Effective Things of None Effect

1 Corinthians 1:17

Introduction

I.   God's ways and plans are effective.

II.   Man can make effective things of none effect.

Discussion

I.   Making the word of God of none effect

    A. Matthew 15:1-6

    B. Mark 7:13

    C. The word of God is true and powerful, yet many are lost. What's the problem? The word is made of none effect.

        1. By lack of faith in the Bible as the word of God (Hebrews 4:2, 11:6; 1 Thessalonians 2:13)

        2. By being ignorant of its teachings (Romans 10:1-3; Hosea 4:6)

        3. By having a hard heart (Matthew 13:13-15)

        4. By following the traditions of men (Matthew 15:1-6; Mark 7:13; Colossians 2:8)

        5. When Satan takes away the word (Luke 8:12)

II. Making Christ of none effect

    A. By trying to be justified by the law of Moses

        1. Galatians 2:21

        2. Galatians 5:4

        3. Christ does have a law (Galatians 6:2).

    B. By refusing to listen to Him

        1. Hebrews 12:25

        2. Matthew 17:5

        3. Acts 3:22

III. Making the cross of Christ of none effect

    A. 1 Corinthians 1:17-18

        1. By preaching the wisdom of men (1 Corinthians 1:17-18)

        2. When men preach that the church is not important (Ephesians 2:16)

        3. Preaching the cross without preaching the resurrection of Christ

            a. Romans 1:4; 1 Peter 3:21; 1 Peter 1:3-4

            b. Many are preaching "the doing and dying of Jesus" and say little if anything about his resurrection!

        4. By preaching the cross without the blood of Christ (Colossians 1:20)

IV. Making God's promises of none effect

    A. Man sinned and God promised salvation through Christ.

        1. Genesis 2 through 3

        2. Genesis 12:1-3

    B. Promise to Abraham fulfilled when one obeys the gospel (Galatians 3:26-29)

    C. How the promise is made of none effect:

        1. By not being in Christ (Galatians 3:27; Ephesians 1:3; 1 John 2:25; 1 John 5:11)

        2. Falling short (Hebrews 4:1, 9; Revelation 2:10)

Conclusion

I.   Obey God's plan, for it is effective.

II.   Be saved by obeying right now.

~ 3 ~
Temporary Things in the Bible

Introduction

I. There are some things in the Bible which God never did intend to be lasting.

    A. A failure to realize this has caused the binding of things which are loosed.

    B. Need for a study in this area.

II. Let's take a look at some of these temporary things.

Discussion

I. God never did intend for the law of Moses to be permanent.

    A. Matthew 5:17

    B. Romans 7:1-4

    C. Hebrews 10:9-10

    D. Galatians 3:16-25

    E. We live by the law of Christ (Galatians 6:2).

II. The apostles

    A. The work of the apostles was temporary.

    B. The word apostle means "one sent."

    C. They were ambassadors for Christ (2 Corinthians 5:20).

D. The qualifications for an apostle shows it to be a temporary office.

    1. Had to be an eye witness of Jesus after his resurrection

    2. Acts 1:22

E. Thus, there are no living apostles today. We don't need any.

III. Spiritual gifts

A. They were bestowed only by an apostle (Acts 8:14-17).

B. We have no living apostles today, thus no one to bestow the gifts!

C. The purpose of spiritual gifts is gone.

    1. The purpose was to confirm the word (Mark 16:15-20; Hebrews 2:2-3).

    2. Keep the church pure so men would not be "carried about by every wind of doctrine" (Ephesians 4:10-16).

    3. The word is no longer in "earthen vessels"—the apostles (2 Corinthians 4:7)—but has been revealed (Jude 3).

D. Spiritual gifts ceased to be operative when the perfect law of liberty—the Word of God—came into existence (1 Corinthians 13:8-10; James 1:25)

IV. The reign of Christ

A. God never did intend for Christ to reign forever.

B. He is reigning now and will until the end of time.

C. 1 Corinthians 15:23-28

D. No such thing as an earthly reign when Christ comes, for it is then He will give up the reign, not begin it!

V. The earth

    A. This earth is temporary.

    B. It will be burned up (2 Peter 3:10).

    C. The hope of God's people is laid up in heaven, not on the earth (Colossians 3:1-2; Matthew 6:10-20; 1 Peter 1:3-4).

VI. Hades

    A. Hades is the realm of departed spirits.

    B. Hades will come to an end at the judgment.

    C. Hades will give up its dead at the judgment (Revelation 20:12-13).

    D. Jesus went to Hades (Acts 2:27).

    E. 2 Peter 2:4

    F. Luke 16:23

VII. Man's earthly life

    A. Man is only here on this earth for a brief period of time.

    B. Life is as grass (1 Peter 1:24).

    C. Man is of few days (Job 14:1-2).

    D. Life is a vapor (James 4:14).

    E. Psalms 103:15

    F. Psalms 90:1-10

    G. Hebrews 9:27

    H. Ecclesiastes 9:5; Romans 5:12

Conclusion

I. Quick review of these seven temporary things

II. Since we are aware of temporary things, let's prepare for eternal things by obeying the gospel as we sing.

~ 4 ~

The Bible Church

Matthew 16:13-20

Introduction

I. There are many things about the Bible church in the word of God.

II. Everything said about the church is so. We just need to study and learn what is said about the church.

Discussion

I. The church is God-planned.

    A. Ephesians 3:10-11

    B. The church is not an afterthought with God but was planned from the beginning.

II. The church is Old Testament-predicted.

    A. The prophets foresaw the coming church.

        1. Isaiah 2:2-3

        2. Micah 4:1-4

        3. Zechariah 1:16

        4. Daniel 2:44

    B. These men were Holy Spirit-guided.

        1. 2 Peter 1:21

2. Thus, they knew whereof they spoke.

III. The Bible church is New Testament-revealed.

   A. Acts 2

   B. Study Acts 2 to show that the church came into existence in the last days as the prophets said it would.

   C. Acts 2:47 shows the church is now in existence.

IV. The Bible church is Christ-built.

   A. The church could not have been built by just anyone.

      1. Psalms 127:1

      2. Vain means empty, or to no avail.

   B. Matthew 16:18

      1. A divine builder

      2. One built by men is not the Bible church!

V. The Bible church is blood-purchased.

   A. Acts 20:28

   B. 1 Corinthians 6:20

   C. 1 Peter 1:18-19

   D. A thing's value can be seen by what it cost. The church was bought with the blood of Christ.

VI. The Bible church is independently organized.

   A. Every church is independent of ever other church.

   B. There are to be elders in every church.

      1. Acts 14:23

      2. Titus 1:5

   C. Philippians 1:1

1. **Elders, deacons** and **members** make up the organization of the church.

2. Christ is the head (Colossians 1:18).

3. The rule of elders begins and ends in the local church (1 Peter 5:1-3).

VII. The Bible church is Christ-possessed.

   A. The church belongs to Christ.

   B. Romans 16:16; Matthew 16:18

   C. The church is identified as to its possession.

VIII. The church is Christ-headed and Christ-subjected.

   A. Everything has to be headed by someone.

   B. Christ is the only head of the church.

      1. Ephesians 1:22, 23

      2. Colossians 1:18

   C. The church must be subject to the head—Christ.

      1. Ephesians 5:24

      2. As physical body and head

Conclusion

I.   Is the church that you are a member of like this church?

II.   Come now by hearing, believing and obeying, and become a member of the Bible church.

~ 5 ~

When God Doesn't Hear

Isaiah 59:1-2

Introduction

I. Read and study the text.

II. There are some times when God does not hear.

Discussion

I. God does not hear the prayer of an alien sinner.

    A. Isaiah 59:1-2

    B. John 9:31

    C. Not in God's family

II. One who regards iniquity in his heart

    A. Psalms 66:18

    B. One's life must be in harmony with his profession.

III. When we have an unforgiving heart

    A. Matthew 6:14-15

    B. Matthew 18:21-35

    C. Make applications.

IV. When husbands mistreat wives

    A. 1 Peter 3:7

      B. Must love as himself (Ephesians 5:22-30)

      C. Discuss and apply.

V.   When our worship is vain

      A. Matthew 15:9

      B. Matthew 4:10; John 4:24

      C. Colossians 2:23

VI.   When Christians fail to meet prayer requirements

      A. In faith (Hebrews 11:6; James 1:5-6)

      B. According to God's will (Matthew 26:39; 1 John 5:14-15)

      C. With right motive (James 4:1-3)

      D. Right spiritual condition (Psalms 66:18; Proverbs 28:9; 1 Peter 3:12)

      E. In the name of Christ (John 14:13-14; Colossians 3:16)

      F. Unselfishly (James 4:3)

VII.   At the judgment when men are lost

      A. Matthew 7:21-23

      B. Matthew 25:1-14. The door was shut. God would not hear their knock nor let them in!

VIII. When our worship is without the true spirit

      A. John 4:24

      B. The spirit is as important as the truth (John 17:17; John 8:32).

      C. We must sing with the spirit and understanding (1 Corinthians 14:15; Colossians 3:16)

Conclusion

I.   We must keep the Lord's commands for Him to hear us.

II.   Obey Him right now while we sing.

~ 6 ~

The Saddest Words in the Bible

Introduction

I.   The Bible contains a long list of sad words. Sad words are often connected with grief.

II. Let's take a look at some of these sad words in the Bible.

Discussion

I.   "Some mocked"

    A. Acts 17:32

    B. Read and study the context of Acts 17:32-34.

    C. It is sad when people will make fun of the resurrection of Christ.

    D. It is sad to mock at the resurrection because:

        1. By the resurrection, Jesus is declared to be the Son of God with power (Romans 1:4).

        2. Baptism saves by the resurrection (1 Peter 3:21)

        3. By the resurrection, men are begotten unto a lively hope (1 Peter 1:3).

II. "We will not walk therein."

    A. Jeremiah 6:16

B. Jeremiah, God's prophet, pleaded for God's people to walk in the old paths. But they, like many today, said, "We will not walk therein." And that's sad.

C. Today, God's people are called upon to walk:

1. In the newness of life (Romans 6:4)

2. In the light (1 John 1:7)

3. By faith (2 Corinthians 5:7)

4. Worthy of our vacation (Ephesians 4:1)

5. In love (Ephesians 5:1-2)

6. Honestly (1 Thessalonians 4:12)

D. It is sad when they say, "We will not walk therein."

III. "Who concerning the truth have erred"

A. 2 Timothy 2:17-18

B. Many have obeyed the truth but have erred, and this is sad.

C. James 5:19

D. 1 Timothy 6:10

E. It is sad because

1. We err from that which makes us free (John 8:32).

2. We leave that which saves us (James 1:21).

3. There is no other way.

IV. "Concerning faith have made shipwreck"

A. 1 Timothy 1:19-20

B. When one has been obedient to the faith and then makes shipwreck of that faith, sad it is.

C. There is no uglier sight to a sailor than a wrecked ship.

D. Many a young person has made shipwreck of their faith.

E. Many do so by:

    1. Having faith overthrown (2 Timothy 2:17-18)

    2. Departing from the faith (1 Timothy 4:1-4)

    3. Denying the faith (1 Timothy 5:8)

    4. By casting off faith (1 Timothy 5:12)

F. Such is sad.

V. "And the door was shut"

    A. Matthew 25:10

    B. It was sad when God shut the door to the ark.

        1. Genesis 7:16

        2. Many were on the outside—left to drown.

    C. Relate the parable of the wise and foolish virgins.

        1. Matthew 25:1-13

        2. These had made some start but failed to stay ready.

        3. Those who were ready went in.

    D. It is sad when men die unprepared to meet God.

    E. The door will never be opened again.

VI. "Depart from Me"

    A. Matthew 25:41

    B. Matthew 7:21-23

    C. Said to those who failed:

        1. To use talents (Matthew 25:30)

        2. To those not benevolent (Matthew 25:41)

        3. To those who fail to obey the Lord (Matthew 7:21-23)

        4. Matthew 25:46

D. Discuss 2 Thessalonians 1:7-9.

E. It will be sad to hear these words.

VII. "Go thy way for this time"

A. Acts 24:25

B. Discuss Acts 24:24-27

C. A sad story because:

1. Felix was so close to the truth.

2. Paul reasoned about righteousness, temperance and judgment. He heard the truth.

3. He never had another opportunity to obey—at least, the record does not reveal it.

VIII. "Almost"

A. Acts 26:28

B. Discuss Paul's defense before Agrippa.

C. Agrippa was a believer (Acts 26:27).

D. Almost is a sad word because:

1. He was almost a Christian.

2. We never read where he had another opportunity to to obey the Lord.

E. Happens to many every day—and that's sad.

F. Don't be almost persuaded, but obey now.

Conclusion

I. These sad conditions do not have to be.

II. You can change them.

A. Do so by obeying the gospel.

B. Come as we sing.

~ 7 ~

Preaching Christ
Acts 8:5

Introduction

I.   It was apostolic practice to preach Christ. To preach Christ is to accept a grave responsibility.

II. Preaching Christ is the only kind of preaching which pleases God.

Discussion

I.   To preach Christ is to preach the Sonship of Jesus.

   A. Acts 9:20

   B. Jesus claimed to be the Son of God.

      1. John 1:1-2

      2. Luke 1:26-35

   C. The resurrection gave proof (Romans 1:4).

II. To preach Christ is to preach the gospel of Christ.

   A. 1 Corinthians 1:23

   B. What did Paul preach?

      1. 1 Corinthians 15:1-6

      2. Jesus had said to preach the gospel (Mark 16:15).

   C. Romans 1:16-17

      1. The gospel is God's power to save.

      2. Contains God's righteousness

III. Preaching Christ involves preaching concerning the kingdom of God.

    A. Acts 8:5

      1. Phillip preached Christ.

      2. In so doing, Paul preached about the kingdom (Acts 8:12).

    B. The kingdom is the church.

      1. In Matthew 16:18 it's called the church, and in verse 19 it's called the kingdom.

      2. Hebrews 12:23, 28

    C. I don't know how one would preach Christ and not teach folks about the church. Do you?

IV. Preaching Christ involves preaching concerning the name.

    A. Often, men pay little attention to the name of Jesus Christ.

    B. Many think one name is as good as another.

      1. Philippians 2:9

      2. Colossians 3:17

    C. Respect for authority is important.

      1. Authority is invested in Jesus Christ.

      2. Matthew 7:29; Matthew 28:18; John 2:5; John 7:46

V. Men and women are baptized when Christ is preached.

    A. The reason folks were baptized in Samaria when Christ was preached is that preaching Christ involves preaching about baptism!

B. Acts 8:5; Acts 8:12; Acts 8:35-36

C. Preachers today claim to be preaching Christ yet never say a word about baptism, except to say that it is not important!

VI.   The preaching of Christ begins with Scripture.

A. Acts 8:35

B. The eunuch was a Bible reader.

C. The eunuch was reading Isaiah 53.

D. 2 Timothy 3:16-17

E. 2 Timothy 3:15

VII.   In preaching Christ, we should begin where the learner is.

A. Acts 8:30-34

B. Philip learned where the eunuch was and began there to teach him.

C. We can ask questions to determine where the learner is.

VIII. To preach Christ, we must open our mouth.

A. Acts 8:35

B. Some preachers have difficulty in opening their mouths in preaching and some have the problem of getting them closed once they get them open.

C. Preachers need to learn that the head can receive no more than the seat can endure.

Conclusion

I.   We need to preach Christ.

II.   Christ-centered sermons bring results.

~ 8 ~
The Father of the Prodigal Son
Luke 15:11-32

Introduction

I.   Perhaps most of the sermons you have heard in regard to the prodigal son have been about the son.

II. This lesson has to do with the father of the prodigal son.

Discussion

I.   The father had a heart of generosity.

   A. The father divided his living with his sons (Luke 15:12).

   B. All the father had belonged to his sons (Luke 15:31).

   C. Generosity is a trait that many never learn.

   D. If God is represented by the father in this story, surely God is a generous father.

      1. God gave us life (Genesis 2:7).

      2. God gave his Son (John 3:16).

      3. James 1:17

      4. God will give us, if faithful, eternal life (1 John 5:11).

II. The father treated his sons kindly.

   A. The son who left home made no accusations against his father.

      B. No harsh treatment was involved in his son's leaving.

      C. He called him father (Luke 15:12).

      D. Some fathers so conduct themselves that it is hard for their sons to call them father.

      E. God is kind.

III.   The father was good to his hired servants.

      A. Luke 15:17-19

      B. Seen by the fact that the boy was willing to go back home as a servant

IV.   The father recognized the free moral agency of his son.

      A. The father did not try to force the boy to stay or return.

          1. The boy made up his own mind.

          2. He came to himself (Luke 15:17).

      B. Our father, God, recognizes the free moral agency of man.

          1. We are free to choose (Joshua 24:15).

          2. There are two roads to choose from (Matthew 7:13-14).

          3. We can come or reject (Matthew 11:28-30).

V.   The father was watching and waiting for his boy to come home.

      A. Luke 15:20

      B. He saw him coming.

      C. Many a father or mother has waited for a wayward son to come home.

      D. God waits the coming of his wayward sons.

VI.   The father had compassion for his son.

    A. Luke 15:20

    B. Our God is a God of compassion.

       1. Psalms 86:15

       2. And Jesus cares (1 Peter 5:7).

       3. Matthew 9:36

       4. 2 Peter 3:9

VII. The father of the prodigal son had a heart of forgiveness.

    A. Luke 15:21-24, 32

    B. The father stood ready to forgive when his son was ready to repent.

    C. He was restored to full sonship.

    D. God restores us to full sonship when we, as his people, return by repenting, confessing our sins and praying for forgiveness.

       1. Acts 8:13-22

       2. 1 John 1:9

    E. God also gives to the alien sinner sonship when he obeys.

       1. Romans 8:15

       2. Galatians 3:26-29

    F. It is as though we had never sinned when we come obeying God.

       1. Sins remembered no more

       2. Hebrews 8:12

    G. When one obeys, brethren must also forgive and forget.

      1. Matthew 18:21-35

      2. God will not forgive us if we don't!

Conclusion

I.   There was joy (Luke 15:24).

II.   There is joy in Heaven when sinners repent and obey God (Luke 15:10).

~ 9 ~

What God Hath Confirmed
Galatians 3:15-18

Introduction

I.   Read and discuss the text.

II.   The meaning of "confirm"

    A. To confirm is to approve to be true.

    B. Sometimes the word is used to mean "to strengthen."

    C. Often we hear of an unconfirmed report.

    D. A thing confirmed cannot:

        1. Be disannulled

        2. Be added to

Discussion

I.   God confirmed the Christ.

    A. Deuteronomy 18:18-19; Acts 3:22-23

    B. John 1:45

    C. John bore witness to the fact (John 1:32-34).

    D. Miracles confirmed Him to be God's Son (John 2:23).

    E. Matthew 17:5

II.   The word of God has been confirmed.

A. Word was confirmed by miracles and signs (Mark 16:15-20).

B. Hebrews 1:1-4

C. Remember, once a thing has been confirmed, it cannot be disannulled or added to (Revelation 22:17-18; 2 John 9). Thus, no need for miracles today to confirm it.

D. Galatians 3:15

III. Souls of the brethren were confirmed.

A. Acts 14:22 (Study the context of Acts 14:19-22.)

B. 1 Corinthians 1:8

C. Acts 15:1-5; Acts 15:24

1. They were confirmed to be free from fleshly circumcision which some were trying to bind on them. For they had been confirmed without fleshly circumcision (Acts 15:32).

D. Galatians 5:1-4

E. Our circumcision is the cutting off of sin (Colossians 2:11).

F. Paul strengthened the disciples (Acts 18:23).

IV. The gospel of Jesus Christ

A. Philippians 1:7

B. The gospel is the power to save (Romans 1:16-17).

1. 1 Corinthians 15:1

2. Ephesians 1:13

C. No need to try to add anything to or change the gospel (Galatians 1:8-9).

1. It has been confirmed.

    2. Needs no gimmicks or rewards—just preach it!

V.   The Lord's church

    A. Acts 14:41

    B. The church has been confirmed and we cannot add to or disannul.

    C. The church does not need any propping up.

    D. We cannot add anything to or disannul:

        1. The head (Colossians 1:18)

        2. The builder (Matthew 16:18)

        3. The organization (Philippians 1:1)

        4. The work (1 Thessalonians 1:8—gospel preaching; 1 Timothy 5:16—benevolence)

        5. The worship (Acts 2:42; Ephesians 5:19; John 4:24)

VI.   The promises of God

    A. Romans 15:8

    B. Galatians 3:14-18

    C. The promises of God were made to Abraham 430 years before the law of Moses, and the law did not make void the promises.

    D. God's promise to Abraham fulfilled in Christ

        1. Galatians 3:16-18

        2. Galatians 3:26-29

            a. Must be baptized into Christ to realize the promise

            b. Mark 16:15-16

Conclusion

I.   A review of what God has confirmed.

II. Remember what God confirms, no man can add to or disannul.

III. Come and obey his confirmed word right now as we sing.

~ 10 ~
The Home as God Would Have It

Introduction

I.   The Bible describes three divine institutions.

    A. The home (Genesis 2:21-24)

    B. The government (Romans 13:1-7)

    C. The church (Matthew 16:18)

II.   The home is important in one's life.

Discussion

I.   Use of the word "home"

    A. A dwelling place (1 Corinthians 11:22, 34)

    B. A corporate body, like an orphan home

    C. The physical body (2 Corinthians 5:6)

    D. The family relationship (1 Timothy 5:4)

II.   The importance of the home

    A. God-founded (Genesis 2:21-24)

    B. As the home goes, so goes the nation.

    C. Psalms 33:12

III.   The place of the man in the home

A. To leave and cleave

   1. Genesis 2:24-25

   2. Must cut the apron strings

   3. Marital responsibilities take a priority over all other family relationships.

   4. Too many parents encourage their children to return home if things don't work out.

B. To love his wife

   1. Ephesians 5:23-25

   2. As Christ loved the church—He gave himself for it.

C. To head up the home

   1. Ephesians 5:23

   2. Some men are too timid to accept this role.

D. To be the father

   1. A man chooses responsibility when he chooses to be a father.

   2. The primary responsibility of child training rests with the father. This is not to say that the mother has none.

   3. Ephesians 6:1-4

   4. Proverbs 13:24

   5. Colossians 3:21

E. To be the breadwinner

   1. 1 Timothy 5:8

   2. Many too lazy (Ephesians 4:28; 2 Thessalonians 3:6-12

F. To bring his children up right

   1. Ephesians 6:4

   2. This is done by training them right.

   3. Teach them, show them, and see that they do it (Proverbs 22:6)!

IV. The place of the woman in the home

A. To be a wife

   1. Genesis 2:18-24

   2. A helpmeet is one who is suitable.

   3. Proverbs 18:22

   4. 1 Corinthians 7:3

   5. 1 Corinthians 11:8-9

B. To be in subjection to her husband

   1. Ephesians 5:22-24

   2. 1 Timothy 2:12

C. To adorn herself modestly

   1. 1 Timothy 2:9-11

   2. 1 Peter 3:1-6

D. To be a teacher of good things

   1. Titus 2:3-5

   2. The teaching is restricted (1 Timothy 2:12).

E. To be a mother

   1. Children are great imitators (Ezekiel 16:44).

   2. It has been said, "The hand that rocks the cradle rules the world."

F. Results of such living

     1. Honored by her husband (1 Peter 3:7)

     2. Her children call her blessed (Proverbs 31:28).

V.   The place of children in the home

    A. I suppose every parent wonders, as did John's parents, "What manner of child shall this be?" (Luke 1:66)

    B. To obey and honor parents

      1. Ephesians 6:1-3

      2. Promotes long life and is right

    C. To hear a father's instruction

      1. Proverbs 4:1; Proverbs 13:1; Proverbs 15:5; Proverbs 10:1

      2. Advice may not be too bad.

    D. Relieve needy parents

      1. 1 Timothy 5:4

      2. 1 Timothy 5:16

    E. Realize the importance of youth

      1. Ecclesiastes 12:1; 1 Timothy 4:12; Titus 1:6-8; 2 Timothy 2:22

      2. Don't misuse your youth.

Conclusion

I.   Realize place and get in it. Then stay in it.

II.   Judges 7:21

~ 11 ~

The Step of Death

1 Samuel 20:3

Introduction

I.   Read and discuss this passage.

II.   We all can say these same words today.

Discussion

I.   The meaning of the word "death"

   A. Death means a separation.

   B. Some examples which show this:

      1. Genesis 2:16-17; Genesis 3:23-24

      2. Luke 15:24

II.   Five ways the word "death" is used in the New Testament

   A. Dead to the law of Moses

      1. Romans 7:1-4

      2. Galatians 2:19

      3. Men are now separated from the law of Moses—thus, no longer under it.

   B. In becoming a sinner

      1. Ephesians 2:1

    2. Man becomes separated from God by his sins (Isaiah 59:1-2).

    3. 1 John 3:4

    4. One may be dead while living (1 Timothy 5:6)!

  C. In becoming a child of God

    1. Dead to sin (Romans 6:1-8)

    2. Colossians 3:3

  D. Physical death

    1. Separating of the body from the spirit

    2. James 2:26

    3. Ecclesiastes 9:5

    4. Luke 23:46

    5. Acts 7:59

  E. The second death

    1. Ezekiel 18:20

    2. A spiritual death (Romans 6:23)

    3. James 1:14-15

    4. Separation (2 Thessalonians 1:7-9)

    5. Revelation 20:12-15

    6. The separating of the spirit from God in Hell is the second death.

III.   Some things the phrase "the step of death" teaches

  A. The brevity of life

    1. Job 7:6

    2. Job 9:25

    3. Job 14:1-2

    4. Psalms 90:9

    5. Psalms 103:15

    6. Psalms 37:25

    7. 2 Corinthians 4:17

    8. 1 Chronicles 29:15

    9. James 4:14

B. A sure step

    1. Ecclesiastes 9:5

    2. 1 Corinthians 15:22

    3. As sure as men live, men will die.

C. An appointed step

    1. Hebrews 9:27

    2. All men will keep this appointment.

D. A common step

    1. Numbers 16:29

    2. All men will die.

    3. Ecclesiastes 9:5; Romans 5:12

E. A separating step

    1. The spirit leaves the body (James 2:26).

    2. Separated from loved ones as well

F. A final step

    1. Death will be the vehicle we will leave this earth on.

    2. After death comes the judgment (Hebrews 9:27).

    3. Death will be the last earthly step we will take.

G. A departing step

       1. 2 Timothy 4:6-8

       2. The words of Paul as he was about ready to die.

    H. A step into eternity

       1. 1 Corinthians 15:36

       2. We must die in order to live.

IV.   States one can die in

    A. In his own sins (John 8:24)

    B. In the displeasure of God (Ezekiel 33:11)

    C. The death of the righteous (Numbers 23:10)

    D. In Christ (Revelation 14:13)

    E. A precious death (Psalms 116:15)

Conclusion

I.   It matters not when we die, as long as we are ready to meet God.

II.   Come today and obey as we sing.

~ 12 ~
Some Things Which Do Not Cover Sin

Romans 4:6-7

Introduction

I. There are some things which do not cover sin.

    A. Some may think that they do.

    B. But that does not make it so.

II. Read and discuss text.

    A. Romans 4:6-7

    B. A quote from Psalms 32:1-2

III. Let's take a look at some things which do not cover sin.

Discussion

I. The blood of bulls and goats does not cover sin.

    A. Hebrews 10:1-4

    B. Hebrews 9:12

    C. Hebrews 10:11

    D. Blood was shed in the Old Testament.

        1. Animal blood was temporary.

        2. Had to offer every year

E. It took the blood of Christ to save men.

    1. Hebrews 9:15; Hebrews 2:9; 1 John 1:7

    2. Romans 5:9; Revelation 1:5

II.   The love of God alone does not cover sin.

    A. It is true that God loves man (John 3:16).

    B. Love alone will not cover sin.

    C. Some think that God loves man too much to allow man to be lost. Ever read Romans 11:22?

III. Geographical space does not cover sin.

    A. One cannot sin and then run off to some other place thinking his sins are forgiven by such an adventure.

    B. Sin is sin wherever one might go (1 John 3:4).

    C. You can't run from sin.

    D. Numbers 32:23

IV. Moral goodness does not cover sin.

    A. This is the thinking of many.

        1. Just be good.

        2. We must be good.

    B. Cornelius was a good, moral man.

        1. Acts 10:2

        2. Yet he was unsaved (Acts 11:14).

    C. It takes more than that.

        1. Matthew 7:21

        2. Luke 6:46

V.   Prayer will not cover alien sins.

    A. John 9:31

   B. Prayer is for the child of God.

      1. Acts 8:13-22

      2. 1 John 1:9

      3. 1 John 5:14

      4. 1 John 3:22

      5. 1 Peter 3:12

   C. Many misapply passages that refer to the Christian's praying.

      1. 1 John 1:9

      2. Written to Christians

VI. Time does not cover sin.

   A. Some seem to think that because man forgets, God will.

   B. Not so

   C. 2 Peter 3:9; Isaiah 55:8-9

   D. Waiting around for men to forget does not cover sin.

   E. Acts 17:30

VII. The confession of sins will not cover alien sins.

   A. Many misapply 1 John 1:9.

      1. Written to Christians

      2. Not to alien sinners

   B. Alien sinners must confess faith in Christ.

      1. Matthew 10:32

      2. Romans 10:9-10

      3. Acts 8:36-37

VIII. Faith alone will not cover sin.

A. Many teach and think so.

B. James 2:14-26

C. Nothing alone will cover sin.

IX. There are some things which do cover sins.

    A. Being converted

        1. James 5:19-20

        2. Men must be changed.

    B. Love covers sins.

        1. 1 Peter 4:8

        2. When men are led to obey (John 14:15, 23).

        3. 1 John 5:2-3

        4. I saw a car bumper sticker which said, "If you love Jesus, wave." The Bible says obey if you love the Lord.

    C. The blood of Christ.

        1. Hebrews 9:22

        2. 1 John 1:9

        3. How does the blood cover sin? Jesus shed his blood in his death (John 19:34) and sinners are baptized into his death (Romans 6:3-4).

Conclusion

I. Some things do not cover sin.

II. Some do.

    A. Let's do those which do cover sin.

    B. Let your love for the Lord lead you to obey. Come now.

~ 13 ~

The Believer in God

1 Peter 1:21-23

Introduction

I. The term "believer in God" is a description of a child of God and what he does because of his relationship to God.

II. Let's study to see who the believer in God is.

Discussion

I. The believer in God believes there is a God.

    A. 1 Peter 1:21

    B. The believer in God has faith in God that He is.

    C. Hebrews 11:6

    D. Genesis 1:1

    E. Only a fool declares there is no God (Psalms 14:1).

II. The believer in God believes in the resurrection of Jesus Christ.

    A. 1 Peter 1:21

    B. Romans 1:4

    C. Acts 2:30

    D. 1 Corinthians 6:14

    E. 1 Thessalonians 1:9-10

F.   Show that the Bible teaches the resurrection.

III.   The believer in God has his faith and hope in God.

    A. People put their faith and hope in about everything else but God.

        1. Money

        2. Men

        3. Things (airplanes, machines, cars, etc.)

    B. 1 Corinthians 2:5

    C. 1 Corinthians 15:19

    D. Psalms 38:15

    E. Psalms 39:7

IV.   The believer in God has a purified soul.

    A. 1 Peter 1:22

    B. The soul in this passage refers to the spirit of man.

    C. How are we purified?

        1. Psalms 119:9

        2. John 15:3

    D. A personal obligation (your soul)

V.   The believer in God is one who has obeyed the gospel.

    A. 1 Peter 1:22

    B. Can't just obey anything but the truth

    C. John 8:32; John 17:17

    D. Romans 6:17-18

    E. Hebrews 5:8-9

    F. Effected by hearing, believing, repenting, confessing and being baptized

VI.   The believer in God is born again.

    A. 1 Peter 1:23

    B. John 3:1-8

    C. The new birth made possible by the word

VII. The believer in God is different from what he was.

    A. 1 Peter 1:1, 13-16

    B. Discuss this passage

    C. Some things the believer in God does:

       1. Girds up the loins of his mind

       2. Is sober

       3. Hopes to the end

       4. Obedient child

       5. Different: does not fashion self according to former lusts

       6. Is holy in manner of life

Conclusion

I.   The believer in God is one who has obeyed the Lord.

    A. Acts 16:34

    B. John 3:36

II.   Come now and obey as we sing.

~ 14 ~

Saved If

1 Corinthians 15:1-4

Introduction

I.   Salvation is conditional: "if"

II. Let's notice some conditions.

Discussion

I.   Saved from past sins if we obey the gospel

    A. Romans 10:16

    B. Romans 6:17-18

    C. What it means to obey the gospel

    D. Mark 16:15; Acts 2:38; Galatians 3:27;
       1 Corinthians 12:13

II. Saved if we keep in memory the things preached

    A. 1 Corinthians 15:1-2

    B. Notice the order: gospel, preached, received (Acts 2:41), stand (Ephesians 6:13-14), saved—*if* we keep in memory things preached. ("To hold on to" is the meaning of keeping in memory.)

    C. 2 Timothy 1:6

    D. 1 Timothy 4:6

III. Saved if we hold fast

    A. Hebrews 3:6

    B. 1 Thessalonians 5:21

    C. 2 Timothy 1:13

    D. Hebrews 4:14

IV.   Saved if we continue in the faith

    A. Colossians 1:22-23

       1. Some do not continue but err from the faith (1 Timothy 6:10).

       2. 2 Timothy 2:18; 1 Timothy 4:1

    B. John 8:31

    C. Acts 2:42

V.   Saved if we walk in the light

    A. 1 John 1:7

    B. Some say that light means love—they love everybody and everything!

    C. To walk in the light is to walk in the word.

    D. Psalms 119:105; Psalms 119:130

VI.   Saved if we abide in the doctrine of Christ

    A. 2 John 9-11

    B. The doctrine of Christ is the teaching of Christ.

    C. Some want to make a distinction between gospel and doctrine. They are the same!

    D. We obey the gospel (Romans 10:16), and we obey doctrine (Romans 6:17-18).

    E. Acts 2:42; 1 Timothy 4:16

VII. Saved if we add these to our faith

    A. 2 Peter 1:5-11

    B. List and discuss each.

VIII. Saved if we endure to the end

    A. Matthew 24:13

    B. Revelation 2:10

    C. 1 Corinthians 15:58

Conclusion

I.   We shall reap if we faint not.

II.   Come now and obey.

~ 15 ~
When We Are Strong
2 Corinthians 12:10; Ephesians 6:10

Introduction

I.   The emphasis men place on strength may not be the same God places on it.

II.   Paul says he was strong when he was being persecuted and when he had infirmities and reproaches for the sake of Christ.

Discussion

I.   We are strong when we have respect for the authority of the Bible.

    A. Colossians 3:17

    B. Numbers 24:13

    C. Ephesians 1:22-23

    D. Matthew 18:18; John 2:5; Matthew 17:5

    E. 2 John 9; 1 Corinthians 4:6

II.   When we are not ashamed of the gospel

    A. Romans 1:16-17

    B. Two reasons: power to save and contains God's righteousness (Romans 10:1-8)

III.   When we are filled with zeal and knowledge

     A. Colossians 1:9

     B. A lack of knowledge kept these from submitting to God's righteousness (Romans 10:1-3).

     C. What you don't know will hurt you.

IV.   When we have burdens to bear

     A. Romans 15:1

     B. Galatians 6:2

     C. 2 Corinthians 12:10

     D. Psalms 119:71

     E. Job 42:5-6

V.   When we practice what we preach

     A. Romans 2:21; Galatians 2:20

     B. 2 Corinthians 3:2; 1 Peter 3:1-3

VI.   When we are united

     A. Psalms 133:1

     B. James 3:16

     C. John 17:20-21; 1 Corinthians 1:1-10; 1 Corinthians 3

Conclusion

I.   Let us strengthen ourselves by doing His will.

II.   Obey His calling today.

~ 16 ~
Five Bible Liars

John 8:44; Colossians 3:9; Revelation 21:8

Introduction

I.   John is best known as the writer of love. The reason is that he often speaks of "the love of God to man, the love of man to God, the love of man to his fellow man."

II.   John also speaks of men who are guilty of lying. Let's take a look at some.

Discussion

I.   Those claiming fellowship with God and walk in darkness

   A. 1 John 1:6

   1. John is saying that if a man claims to be of God with his lips and then in turn lives a life that is not of God, he is a liar.

   2. Why such a man is a liar: he is guilty of contradicting his claims by his living, and he is proven to be a liar.

   3. When members here claim to be in fellowship with God by their lips but fail to practice what He commands in living, claiming one thing on Sunday and living another during the week—such are *liars*.

   a. Claim to be a child and fail to pray

(1 Thessalonians 5:17-18)

    b. Fail to give (1 Corinthians 16:1-2)

    c. Fail to attend (Hebrews 10:25)

II.   Claiming to know God and not obeying His commands

    A. 1 John 2:4

    B. John is here teaching that if a person claims to be of God but will not listen to what God says, he is a liar.

    C. Notice some of his commands:

        1. Repent and be baptized (Acts 2:28)

        2. Sing (Hebrews 2:12)

III.   The man that denies that Jesus is the Christ is a liar.

    A. 1 John 2:22-23

    B. Some think they have to express aloud they do not believe.

        1. Must believe (John 8:24; Hebrews 11:6)

        2. Believe all things he has commanded (Luke 6:46; Matthew 7:21)

IV.   Claims to love God and hates his brother

    A. 1 John 4:20-21

    B. It is impossible for a man to love God and at the same time hate his brother. Whenever a man claims to be a child of God and fails to speak to his brother, *he is a liar!* (John 3:16; 1 Corinthians 13)

        1. It is true that I may dislike the ways of some people, but I must never let hatred get into my heart; if so, then I fail to love God, and I am a liar!

V.   Those who add to the word

A. Proverbs 30:6

B. We are admonished throughout the word of God to leave it as written (Deuteronomy 4:2; 1 Corinthians 4:6; 2 John 9; Revelation 22:18-19)

C. Adding of things not authorized

    1. Instrumental music in worship

    2. Voting on candidates

    3. Counting beads

    4. Unscriptural organization to do the work (1 Timothy 4:1-5)

Conclusion

I. Remember, liars will not go to Heaven (Revelation 21:8).

II. Be truthful and obey the Lord.

~ 17 ~
Choose Ye This Day
Joshua 24:14

Introduction

I.   Man has always been faced with the task of making decisions.

   A. Adam and Eve (Genesis 2:16-17; Genesis 3:1-6)

   B. Moses (Hebrews 11:23)

   C. Joshua (Joshua 24:15)

Discussion

I.   Choose between right and wrong.

   A. Isaiah 7:16

   B. Deuteronomy 1:39

   C. Hebrews 5:12-14

   D. Colossians 3:25

   E. Need to study to know and do

II. Choose the God of the Bible

   A. 1 Kings 18:21

   B. Joshua 24:15

   C. Exodus 20:3; Matthew 4:10; Ephesians 4:5

   D. Acts 17:28

III. Choose that good part.

   A. Luke 10:38-42

   B. Relate the story.

   C. Choose to hear the word of God (Acts 13:7).

   D. Some reasons for this choice

      1. Produces faith (Romans 10:17)

      2. Saves (Acts 11:14; James 1:21)

      3. Builds up and gives an inheritance (Acts 20:32)

   E. Psalms 1

IV. Choose a good name.

   A. Proverbs 22:1

   B. A son and daughter ought not to do things which will dishonor their good name.

   C. The name Christian (Acts 11:26; Acts 26:28; 1 Peter 4:16)

   D. James 2:7

V. Choose to serve God over pleasures for a season.

   A. Moses (Hebrews 11:23-28)

   B. Pleasures only for a season—serving God forever!

VI. Choose to be a Christian.

   A. A simple process: H, R, B, C, B

   B. Also a member of the church

VII. Choose life.

   A. Deuteronomy 30:19; 1 Peter 3:10

   B. Romans 6:23; 1 Peter 5:11

VIII. Choices which determine our destiny (Matthew 7:13-14)

A. Two gates: straight/broad

B. Two ways: wide/narrow

C. Two groups: many/few

D. Two destinies: life/destruction

E. Two foundations: rock/sand (Matthew 7:21-24)

F. Two kinds of righteousness: man's/God's (Romans 10:1-3; Acts 10:34-35; Psalms 119:172)

G. Two deaths to die: in sin/in the Lord (John 8:24; Revelation 14:13)

Conclusion

I. Choose this day

A. The Bible places emphasis on today.

B. 2 Corinthians 6:2

C. Hebrews 3:7, 13-19

D. Proverbs 27:1

II. Decide right now to be a child of God as we sing.

~ 18 ~
Things Not Found in Hell
Luke 16:19-31

Introduction

I. Too often the subject of Hell is treated too lightly. Some say, "Don't tell people there is a Hell."

II. Preaching on Hell may have cooled down, but Hell has not!

Discussion

I. There is a Hell.

    A. Psalms 9:17

    B. Matthew 5:22

    C. Matthew 13:24-42

    D. Matthew 25:31-46

    E. Mark 9:43-48; Jude 7

    F. 2 Peter 2:4; 2 Thessalonians 1:7-10

    G. Hebrews 10:26-32; Revelation 14:10

    H. Revelation 20:11-15; Revelation 21:8

II. Who is going to Hell?

    A. The alien sinner

        1. Matthew 7:21

        2. 1 Peter 4:17; 2 Thessalonians 1:7-9

    B. The hypocrite

        1. Matthew 23:13-15

        2. Luke 6:46

    C. The lukewarm Christian

        1. Revelation 3:15-16

        2. Such is distasteful to God.

    D. Those in Revelation 21:8

    E. Those who add to the word of God

        1. Matthew 25:30

        2. Revelation 22:18-20

III.   Some things not found in Hell

    A. There is no light in Hell.

        1. Matthew 25:30

        2. We would go blind in about 8 days in total darkness!

    B. No mercy in Hell

        1. Luke 16:24

        2. Matthew 5:7; Titus 3:5

        3. Take advantage of it here!

    C. No water supply

        1. Luke 16:24

        2. One drop of water welcome

        3. Water is essential to life and food development.

    D. No earthly possessions

        1. Luke 16:25

        2. 1 John 2:15; Job 1:1

3. Luke 12:16-21; 1 Timothy 6:7

E. No transportation

1. Luke 16:26

2. We are accustomed to going!

3. Confinement for life is second worst punishment.

4. Does away with theory of purgatory.

F. No communication

1. Luke 16:27

2. No contact with the dead

G. No desire for friends or company

1. Luke 16:28

2. "If so and so goes, I want to go."

H. No unbelievers or infidels in Hell

1. Isaiah 45:23

2. Romans 14:11

3. Philippians 2:10

I. No faithful Christians in Hell

1. Revelation 2:10

2. 2 Timothy 4:8

IV. How to keep from going

A. Obey the gospel

B. Live a Christian life

Conclusion

I. Come now

II. Obey

~ 19 ~

Meeting My Responsibilities

Ecclesiastes 12:13-14

Introduction

I.   Men and women have many responsibilities in a number of areas.

II.   Yet many look upon them very lightly.

Discussion

I.   Responsibilities to God

    A. Fear God

        1. Ecclesiastes 12:13-14

        2. To fear God is to respect God (Acts 10:23-35).

    B. Love God

        1. Matthew 22:37-38

        2. God loved us (John 3:16)

    C. Obey God

        1. Ecclesiastes 12:13-14

        2. Hebrews 5:8-9

        3. Acts 5:29

    D. Worship God

        1. John 4:24

II.   Responsibilities to Christ

    A. Keep his commandments.

        1. John 14:15; John 14:23

        2. Luke 6:46; Matthew 7:21

    B. Be in subjection to Him.

        1. Ephesians 5:22-25

        2. He is head (Colossians 1:18).

    C. Believe that He is the Son of God.

        1. John 8:24

        2. John 20:30-31

III.   Responsibilities to the church

    A. Attend the services of the church.

        1. Hebrews 10:25

        2. Faithful

    B. Support with your money.

        1. 1 Corinthians 16:1-2

        2. 2 Corinthians 9:6-7

    C. Be a part of it.

        1. Some act as if they were not a part of it.

        2. "They" instead of "we"

        3. 1 Corinthians 12:14-17

IV.   Responsibilities to others

    A. Teach

        1. 2 Timothy 2:2

        2. Only way folks are converted

    B. Restore the fallen

        1. Galatians 6:1

        2. A great need

    C. Exhort and encourage

        1. Hebrews 10:25

        2. Hebrews 3:11

V.   Responsibilities to my family

    A. Children

        1. Bring up in the nurture and admonition of the Lord (Ephesians 6:4).

        2. Include discipline (Proverbs 22:6).

    B. Wife or husband

        1. Love (Ephesians 5:22; Titus 2:3-5)

        2. Render due benevolence (fulfill his duty) (1 Corinthians 7:5)

        3. Honor and respect (Ephesians 5:33; 1 Peter 3:7)

    C. Provide for

        1. 1 Timothy 5:8

VI.   Responsibilities to self

    A. Obey and work out own salvation.

        1. 1 Timothy 4:16

    B. Examine

        1. 2 Corinthians 13:5

    C. Take heed

        1. Philippians 2:12

Conclusion

I. Live up to your responsibilities to yourself and to God.

II. Only you can make these types of decisions; search your heart. Come, obey as we sing.

~ 20 ~
What Is Man That Thou Art Mindful of Him
Hebrews 2:6; Psalms 8:3-4

Introduction

I.   Our lesson is divided into two part:

   A. What is man?

   B. God's mindfulness of man

II.   We appeal to the scriptures to answer.

Discussion

I.   What is man?

   A. Man is composed of two parts:

      1. Body (Genesis 2:7; Ecclesiastes 12:7; 2 Corinthians 5:10)

      2. Spirit (Genesis 2:7; Ecclesiastes 12:7; Matthew 16:26; 2 Corinthians 5:1-4)

   B. Man is a sinner.

      1. Romans 3:9-10; Romans 3:23

      2. 1 John 3:4

      3. 1 John 5:17

      4. Romans 6:23; James 1:15

C. Man is a dying individual.

   1. Ecclesiastes 9:5

   2. 1 Corinthians 15:22

   3. Hebrews 9:27

D. Man is of few days.

   1. Job 14:1

   2. Job 7:6

   3. 1 Samuel 20:3

   4. Psalms 102:15

   5. Psalms 90:9

   6. James 4:14

E. Man's life is the target of Satan.

   1. Genesis 3

   2. 1 Peter 5:8

   3. 2 Corinthians 2:11

F. Man is the object of God's love.

   1. John 3:16

   2. Romans 5:8

G. Man is one with duty and purpose to glorify God.

   1. Ecclesiastes 12:13-14

   2. 1 Peter 4:16

II. God's mindfulness of man

A. God wants none to be lost

   1. Ezekiel 33:11

   2. 1 Timothy 2:3-4

      3. 2 Peter 3:9

  B. Established the church

      1. Matthew 16:18; Acts 20:28; Ephesians 3:10-11

      2. Saved in it (Acts 2:47)

  C. Gave man the plan of salvation

      1. Hear, believe, repent, confess, be baptized.

      2. Be faithful (Revelation 2:10).

  D. Gave us a book by which to live

      1. Titus 2:11-12

      2. 2 Peter 1:3; 2 Timothy 3:16-17

  E. Given us warnings

      1. 1 Peter 4:17-18

      2. John 12:48

      3. 2 Thessalonians 1:7-9

      4. Mark 13:32-36

  F. Has eternal life for us

      1. 2 Timothy 4:6-8

      2. 1 Peter 1:4

      3. Revelation 2:10

      4. Matthew 25:46

Conclusion

I.   You have learned that God does care about man, that he is mindful of us all.

II.   Why not obey Him right now?

~ 21 ~

In the Church

Introduction

I.   I would like to emphasize the phrase "in the church" in our lesson.

II. We can learn some lessons from this expression.

Discussion

I.   The saved are in the church.

    A. Acts 2:47

    B. Ephesians 5:23

II. Elders in every church

    A. Acts 14:23

    B. Titus 1:3

    C. Philippians 1:1

III. Singing to be done in the church

    A. Hebrews 2:12; Psalms 22:22

    B. Vocal music authorized for the worship in the church (Ephesians 5:19; Colossians 3:16)

IV. Paul's attitude toward tongue speaking in the church

    A. 1 Corinthians 14:19

  B. Yet some try to speak in tongues today—ceased (1 Corinthians 13:8).

  C. A tongue in the Bible was a language men could understand (Acts 2:1-11)

V. Our coming together is to be in the church.

  A. 1 Corinthians 14:23

  B. 1 Corinthians 11:18-22

  C. Study context of Hebrews 10:25

VI. Some set in the church

  A. 1 Corinthians 12:28

  B. God began things with a miracle, like in the beginning when man was created full-grown.

VII. Shame for a woman to speak in the church

  A. 1 Corinthians 14:34-35

  B. Assembly

  C. Passage that would apply to other times (1 Timothy 2:12)

VIII. Word of God to be read in church

  A. Colossians 4:16

  B. Revelation 1:3

  C. 1 Timothy 4:16

IX. God to be glorified in the church

  A. Ephesians 3:21

  B. 1 Peter 4:16

  C. Matthew 5:13-16

    D. Not that the church is to get the glory, as many seem to believe

X.   Those in the church or kingdom to be delivered to God

    A. 1 Corinthians 15:24; Revelation 1:9

    B. Must be in it while we live

Conclusion

I.   Won't you be a part of the Lord's church while you have an opportunity?

II.   Come and accept His call today.

~ 22 ~
The Two Salvations
Romans 13:11

Introduction

I.   Many have failed to understand that the Bible uses the word "salvation" in two senses.

   A. Salvation from past sins

   B. Salvation in Heaven

II. The consequences of this misunderstanding has led some to believe that one has eternal life here and now and cannot lose it.

Discussion

I.   Salvation from past sins

   A. Man becomes a sinner.

       1. Romans 3:23; Ezekiel 28:15; Isaiah 7:16; Mark 10:14; Matthew 18:1-3

       2. 1 John 3:4—Sins in lawlessness

   B. Christ died for sinners.

       1. Luke 19:10; John 3:16; Matthew 1:21

       2. 1 Timothy 1:15; Romans 5:8

   C. God's plan for saving man

       1. Matthew 28:18-20

    2. Mark 16:15-16

    3. Hebrews 5:8-9; Romans 6:17-18

D. The plan preached and obeyed

    1. Acts 2:1-47

    2. Acts 8:26-40

E. This salvation depends on faith.

    1. Hebrews 11:6

    2. John 8:24

    3. Romans 5:1

    4. Acts 2:36

    5. Acts 16:30-31

II.   Salvation that is future—in Heaven

A. Told how to get pardon

    1. Repent and pray (Acts 8:13-22)

    2. Confess sin (1 John 1:9)

B. Salvation yet future

    1. 1 Peter 1:5

    2. 1 Peter 1:9; Titus 1:2; 1 John 2:25

    3. Hebrews 9:28

    4. Romans 5:9-10

    5. Acts 15:11

    6. Romans 13:11

    7. 1 Thessalonians 5:8-9

    8. Philippians 2:12

    9. Hebrews 1:14

        10. 1 Corinthians 3:15

        11. 1 Corinthians 5:5; Romans 6:22; Mark 10:30

        12. 1 Timothy 4:16; Romans 2:7-8

  C. Salvation in Heaven depends on our faith.

     1. Out of the 27 books of the New Testament, 21 are written to tell Christians how to live in order to receive salvation in Heaven.

     2. There are more than 20 passage that show our salvation depends upon our faith.

     3. Hebrews 3:12-14

     4. Hebrews 4:1

     5. Hebrews 20:38

     6. 1 Corinthians 9:27

     7. 1 Timothy 4:16; Romans 2:7-8

     8. Romans 1:17; 2 Corinthians 5:7

  D. Look what can happen to our faith.

     1. May fail (Luke 22:32)

     2. Shipwreck (1 Timothy 1:19)

     3. May depart from (1 Timothy 4:1)

     4. Can deny it (1 Timothy 5:8)

     5. May cast it off (1 Timothy 5:11-12)

     6. May err from it (1 Timothy 6:20-21)

     7. May overthrow it (2 Timothy 2:16-18)

Conclusion

I.   Obey the gospel for salvation from past sins.

II.   Live a faithful life for salvation in Heaven (Revelation 2:10).

~ 23 ~
These Are Precious
(A Series)

Introduction

I.   A number of things are said to be precious in the Bible.

    A. The word precious, as used in the Bible, means "that which is very costly and of great value."

    B. Many misuse the word precious.

II. A number of things are said to be precious—thus, we take a look.

Discussion

I.   The word of the Lord

    A. 1 Samuel 3:1

    B. The circumstances: God had not spoken for a long time. The word was precious.

    C. A famine of hearing the word of the Lord (Amos 8:11)

    D. Too many take the word of God for granted.

        1. Never read and study it

        2. 2 Timothy 2:15; 1 Timothy 4:13; Revelation 1:3

    E. Some reasons the word is precious

        1. Spoke the world into existence (Hebrews 11:3; Genesis 1)

      2. Guided the prophets of old (2 Peter 1:16-21)

      3. Led the people of God in Old Testament times (Hebrews 1:2)

      4. God inspired (2 Timothy 3:16-17)

      5. Reveals God's righteousness (Romans 1:17)

      6. Saves the souls of men (James 1:21)

II. Christ is precious.

    A. 1 Peter 2:4-8

    B. Christ is not precious to all men (Isaiah 53:1-12; 1 Peter 2:8).

    C. He is precious to those who believe (1 Peter 2:7).

    D. Precious because:

      1. Lived a humble life (Matthew 8:20)

      2. Set a perfect example (1 Peter 2:21)

      3. Was obedient (Hebrews 6:8-9)

      4. Is man's savior (Ephesians 5:23)

III. The blood of Christ is precious.

    A. 1 Peter 1:18-19

    B. Life is in the blood (Leviticus 17:11; Genesis 9:4).

    C. Hebrews 9:22

    D. Blood stands for the cost of human redemption.

      1. 1 Peter 1:18-19

      2. Hebrews 9:22

      3. Matthew 26:26-28

      4. 1 John 1:7

      5. Hebrews 9:15

E. Some things the blood does:

   1. Romans 5:9

   2. Ephesians 5:9

   3. Colossians 1:25

   4. Ephesians 2:13

IV. Precious faith

  A. 2 Peter 2:1

  B. Discuss how faith comes (Romans 10:17)

  C. There is one faith (Ephesians 4:41)

  D. Gospel is the faith (Galatians 1:22, 23; 1 Corinthians 15:2)

V. Precious substance

  A. Proverbs 12:27

  B. Proverbs 3:9

  C. Compare the slothful and the diligent man.

  D. One who by honesty and industry acquires substance has God's blessings, and it is called precious substance.

  E. Job 1:3,10

  F. Job 5:5

  G. Job 6:22

  H. Luke 15:13

  I. Man must obtain his substance right.

   1. Ephesians 4:28; 1 Thessalonians 4:11-12; 2 Thessalonians 3:10-12

   2. Any honest occupation

  J. Man has responsibility toward his substance.

    1. Old Testament: Deuteronomy 14:22, 27-29; Leviticus 23:32-33; Malachi 3:10

    2. New Testament: 1 Corinthians 16:1-2; 2 Corinthians 9:6-7; Acts 20:35; Luke 6:38

VI. Precious seed

    A. Psalms 126:5-6

    B. We often sing

        1. "Bringing in the Sheaves"

        2. "Scattering Precious Seed"

    C. The precious seed is the word of God (Luke 8:11; 1 Peter 1:23).

    D. Must be sown (Luke 8:5-15; John 4:35-36; Matthew 9:37-38)

    E. Soil must be right.

VII. Precious unity

    A. Psalms 133:1-3

    B. Discuss the text.

    C. John 17:20-21; 1 Corinthians 1:10-13; 1 Corinthians 12:14-25

    D. Unity achieved (Ephesians 4:1-6)

VIII. Precious trial of faith

    A. 1 Peter 1:7

    B. Trying of our faith is important (James 1:3).

    C. God sometimes makes a test of our faith (Hebrews 11:17; Genesis 22).

    D. Results of being tried and found faithful (James 1:12)

IX. Precious promises

    A. 2 Peter 1:4

    B. A promise is a pledge to do or not to do.

    C. God's promises are bestowed by His divine power (2 Peter 1:3).

    D. God's promises are true.

        1. For God cannot lie (Hebrews 6:18; 1 Kings 8:56; Hebrews 10:23)

        2. God means what He says and says what He means (Hebrews 2:1-4)!

    E. Some general promises of God

        1. Promise of the Savior (Genesis 3:15)

        2. Promise to Abraham (Genesis 12:1-3; Genesis 15:1-6)

        3. Bow in the cloud (Genesis 9:11-17)—no more floods to destroy the world

    F. Promise of rest to the weary

        1. Matthew 11:28-30

        2. Psalms 50:15

        3. Hebrews 6:10-11

        4. Hebrews 4:1, 9

    G. Promise of salvation from past sins

        1. Mark 16:16

        2. Acts 2:38; Acts 22:16; 1 Peter 3:21

    H. Some promises to Christians

        1. All spiritual blessings (Ephesians 1:3)

    2. Promise to hear our prayers (1 John 5:14; Philippians 4:6; 1 John 3:22)

    3. Promise to return for his own (2 Peter 3:4-10)

    4. Promise of life (1 Timothy 1:1; 1 Timothy 4:8; James 1:12; James 2:5; Revelation 2:10; Titus 1:2)

I. Some promises to the alien sinner

    1. Punishment (2 Thessalonians 1:7-9)

    2. Wrath (Romans 2:6-8)

    3. Second death (Revelation 20:14-15)

X. Precious death

    A. Psalms 116:15

    B. A saint is a Christian (1 Corinthians 1:1-2; Philippians 1:1)

    C. The word death means separation.

        1. Genesis 2:16-17

        2. Luke 15:24, 32

        3. James 2:26

    D. Physical death

        1. Physical death is when the spirit separates from the body (James 2:26).

        2. Ecclesiastes 9:5; 1 Corinthians 15:22; Romans 5:12; Hebrews 9:27

    E. Spiritual death

        1. Spiritual death is when man's spirit is separated from God.

        2. Ezekiel 18:20

        3. Romans 6:23

    4. James 1:13-15

    5. Revelation 20:12-15

F. When death is precious

    1. When a person is a saint (Psalms 116:15)

    2. When a person dies in the Lord (Revelation 14:13)

    3. To die in the Lord, one must be in Him (Galatians 3:27).

Conclusion

I. Review all points.

II. Are these things precious to you? If not, come and obey right now.

~ 24 ~
Lessons Preachers Can Learn From Paul
1 Corinthians 2:1-5

Introduction

I.   Most of us who preach could profit in our preaching by learning some things of the preaching of Paul.

II.   Let's notice some of these things.

Discussion

I.   Paul was consistent in his preaching.

    A. Paul taught the same things everywhere (1 Corinthians 4:17).

    B. 1 Corinthians 7:17

    C. Many preachers are inconsistent.

    D. Truth is consistent with truth.

II.   Paul was not ashamed of the gospel of Christ.

    A. Romans 1:16-17

    B. He preached the gospel.

       1. 1 Corinthians 15:16

       2. Romans 1:15

       3. 1 Corinthians 9:16

    4. 1 Corinthians 1:23

    5. He preached the whole counsel of God (Acts 20:27).

C. Many today seem to be ashamed of the gospel.

    1. Many preachers do not really "bear down."

    2. The gospel is the only power we have. Use it!

III. Paul preached with simplicity.

A. 2 Corinthians 11:3

B. 1 Corinthians 2:1-7

C. Preaching must be so folks can understand it.

    1. Ephesians 3:4

    2. 1 Corinthians 14:9, 19

D. Never did anyone say in the New Testament as they listened to preaching, "I don't understand it!"

E. One elder told me, "We are looking for a preacher who will send us to the dictionary." Looks like they needed one who would send them to the Bible!

IV. Paul was humble in his preaching.

A. Acts 20:19

B. 1 Corinthians 4:4

C. Too many preachers are haughty.

D. The Bible teaches us to be humble. Someone said, "If you don't believe our preacher can preach, you just ask him."

    1. James 4:6

    2. 1 Peter 5:6

    3. Galatians 6:1

V. Paul preached the whole counsel of God.

A. Acts 20:27

B. Some seem to be afraid to preach all of the gospel.

C. We must.

    1. 2 Timothy 4:2

    2. Results (Acts 20:26)

D. A preacher doesn't need a "friend" in the audience when he preaches!

VI.   Paul didn't preach to please men.

A. Galatians 1:10

B. 2 Timothy 2:1-4

C. Many today would rather preach to please men than God.

D. We must speak as the oracles of God (1 Peter 4:11).

VII. Paul believed what God had to say.

A. Acts 27:25

B. Read and discuss Acts 27:7-44.

C. We need to have faith in God (Hebrews 11:6).

D. 2 Timothy 1:12

VIII. Paul practiced what he preached.

A. He showed them and then taught them (Acts 20:20).

B. Many preachers want to do a lot of teaching but little practicing.

C. Romans 2:21-22

D. Jesus did and then taught (Acts 1:1).

E. Ezra 7:10—Notice the order: he first did and then taught. So must we.

F. 2 Timothy 4:6-8

Conclusion

I. Preachers can profit by studying the life and preaching of this great apostle.

II. Those who need to obey the Lord are now invited to come.

~ 25 ~
Shame on You

Introduction

I.   A parent, in trying to get a child not to do something, will sometimes say, "Shame on you."

II.   The Bible uses the expression to express God's disfavor with things we may do. Let's take a look at some to whom God says, "Shame on you."

Discussion

I.   Those not having the knowledge of God

    A. 1 Corinthians 15:34

    B. Some don't want to have the knowledge of God (Romans 1:28).

    C. We need to know about God.

        1. That He is our creator (Genesis 2:7)

        2. The sustainer of life (Acts 17:28)

        3. The one to be feared and obeyed (Ecclesiastes 12:13-14)

    D. Thus, we have the need for study (Revelation 1:3).

II.   Going to law with a brother in Christ

    A. 1 Corinthians 6:1-8

B. Bad influence is left with the world when brethren cannot get along.

C. Rather take wrong, if need be.

III. Some things which are spoken

    A. Ephesians 5:11-12

    B. Discuss these sins.

    C. There are some sins men commit that are too bad to discuss before others.

IV. Those who refuse instructions

    A. Proverbs 13:18

    B. Some will just not listen to instructions and advice.

    C. Jesus had this problem in His day (Matthew 13:15).

    D. We need to listen

        1. Children to parents (Proverbs 13:1)

        2. Men to God (Matthew 17:5); through Christ (Hebrews 1:1-2)

        3. Galatians 6:1

V. Those who answer a matter before hearing

    A. Proverbs 18:13

    B. Problem here: One may not have all of the evidence.

    C. Results: Give the wrong answer.

    D. This is very true concerning scripture.

        1. Read all on a given subject.

        2. Then you can arrive at the truth.

VI. The lazy

    A. Proverbs 10:5

   B. Some are too lazy to work.

    1. Hebrews 6:12

    2. 2 Thessalonians 3:6-15

    3. Those too lazy to work shouldn't eat!

   C. We are admonished to work.

    1. John 9:4

    2. 1 Thessalonians 4:11-12

    3. Ephesians 4:28

VII. A child left to himself brings shame.

   A. Proverbs 29:15

   B. This is the lot of many young folks today.

   C. Many children are left to grow up as they please with no restraints.

   D. Many parents bring on their own problems with their children.

VIII. Those who mind earthly things

   A. Philippians 3:19-20

   B. Colossians 3:1-2

   C. Matthew 6:19-20

   D. This affects lots of church members.

    1. Keeps folks from attending as they should (Hebrews 10:25)

    2. Hinders their giving as prospered (1 Corinthians 16:2)

    3. Makes folks worldly (Romans 12:1-2)

Conclusion

I.   What would the Lord say to you about these things?

II.   Come now as we sing to obey.

~ 26 ~
Before and After Faith Came
Galatians 3:23-29

Introduction

I.   So many misunderstand this subject.

II.   One of the most important lessons that men need to learn

    A. The word "faith" here means the gospel.

    B. Galatians 1:23; 1 Corinthians 15:2

Discussion

I.   Before faith, men were under the law—after faith, the law of Christ.

    A. Galatians 3:23

    B. Colossians 2:14

    C. Galatians 6:2

    D. Hebrews 9:16-17

II.   Before faith, only the Jews—now, worldwide

    A. Matthew 10:5-6

    B. Deuteronomy 5:3

    C. After faith

        1. Mark 16:15-16

        2. Matthew 28:19-20

      3. Galatians 3:28

III.   Fleshly circumcision—circumcision of the heart

    A. Before faith

       1. Genesis 17:10-11

       2. Acts 15:1

       3. Romans 2:25-27

    B. After faith

       1. Romans 2:28-29

       2. Philippians 3:3-4

       3. Colossians 2:11-13

       4. Galatians 5:6

IV.   Jerusalem the place of worship—physical place not bound

    A. John 4:19-22

    B. Acts 8:26

    C. John 4:23-24

    D. No longer bound to Jerusalem but in spirit and in truth

V.   Animal sacrifices—living sacrifice

    A. Hebrews 10:8

    B. Hebrews 10:1-4

    C. Romans 12:1-3

    D. Sacrifices are now spiritual, not that of an animal.

VI.   Sins remembered annually—remembered no more

    A. Before faith, sins were remembered (Hebrews 10:1-4)

       1. The blood of animals could not take away sins.

       2. A temporary arrangement until Christ died.

B. Hebrews 10:17-18

   1. Under the gospel, sins forgiven are forgotten.

   2. Should be happy that we are under the gospel

VII. Sabbath kept—first day of the week

  A. Exodus 20:8

  B. Acts 20:7; 1 Corinthians 16:1-2

  C. Discuss the points as time permits.

VIII. Types and shadows—the true

  A. Hebrews 10:1

  B. Hebrews 9:23-24

  C. Now we have the real thing, since faith has come.

Conclusion

I. Have you obeyed the faith?

  A. Acts 6:7; Romans 10:16

  B. Hear, believe, repent, confess the Lord, be baptized

II. Come right now as we sing.

~ 27 ~
Lovers of the Bible I

Introduction

I. This is not a sermon on romance. It does deal with a list of things we should and should not love.

II. A failure to have the proper love for right things is a major cause of people neglecting their responsibilities.

Discussion

I. Lovers of God

  A. God expects first place in the lives of His people.

    1. Matthew 22:37

    2. 2 Timothy 3:4

  B. Some seem to find no pleasure in loving God (Romans 1:28).

  C. We should be as Peter (John 21:15).

II. Lovers of good

  A. God expects us to be lovers of good men and good things.

    1. Titus 1:8

    2. A qualification for elders

    B. We need to think on the good (Philippians 4:8).

    C. Men must learn the difference in good and evil (Hebrews 5:14).

III. Lovers of hospitality and strangers

    A. Many fail to practice hospitality.

    B. The Lord commands us to practice it.

       1. Titus 1:8

       2. 1 Peter 4:9

       3. Romans 12:13

    C. Too many just do not want to clean up the mess, an afternoon nap, and are too lazy to practice hospitality.

    D. Christians must be a willing host without partiality.

IV. Lovers of the brethren

    A. There is just not enough love among the brethren.

    B. Romans 12:10

    C. Hebrews 13:1

    D. 1 Peter 1:22

    E. It is high time that we practice these principles.

V. Lovers of worldly wisdom

    A. We must beware of the "god of education." Education is fine, but there are some dangers in too much learning.

    B. Paul warned the Colossians.

       1. Colossians 2:8

       2. We must not let philosophy spoil us.

    C. We must not think too highly of men.

       1. 1 Corinthians 2:5

2. 1 Corinthians 4:6

D. Gospel preaching must not be with "enticing words of men's wisdom" (1 Corinthians 2:4).

E. Man cannot know God nor His will by worldly wisdom.

F. 1 Corinthians 1:25

VI. Lovers of pleasure

A. 2 Timothy 3:4

B. We are living in a "pleasure crazy" world.

C. 1 Timothy 5:6

D. Loving pleasure keeps many from obeying the Lord.

1. Luke 8:14

2. We must keep our love in the proper order.

E. Pleasures of sin last only for a season (Hebrews 11:25).

VII. Lovers of the truth

A. The truth is the word of God (John 17:17).

B. We must love it (Psalms 119:127).

C. Loving the truth is a matter of life and death (2 Thessalonians 2:10).

D. A failure to love the truth keeps people from obeying it (John 14:15, 23).

Conclusion

I. It is important that we love the right things in the right way.

II. We need to love the Lord and His word enough to obey. Come right now, believing and obeying as we sing.

~ 28 ~
Lovers of the Bible II

Introduction

I.   Review briefly "Lovers of the Bible" lesson.

II.   We continue to look at lovers which are mentioned in the Bible.

    A. We are not discussing romance...

    B. ...but vital lessons about Bible love.

Discussion

I.   Lovers of self

    A. 2 Timothy 3:1-2

        1. This is being fulfilled.

        2. Being so much in love with self, many have no room for loving God.

    B. John 12:25

    C. The love for self has led many to gratify their own desires, regardless of what God has said.

II.   Lovers of money

    A. 1 Timothy 6:10

        1. Money is not the problem but the love of it.

      2. 1 Timothy 6:17

   B. Money must be obtained and used properly.

III. Lovers of the praise of men

   A. Some are more concerned about what men think than God.

   B. John 12:43

   C. Paul's attitude (Galatians 1:10)

   D. When we seek to please men, we have the reward when men are pleased (Matthew 23).

IV. Lovers of the world

   A. Christians are admonished not to love the world (1 John 2:15-17).

   B. Notice what it did to Demas (2 Timothy 4:10).

   C. James 4:4

   D. There is not conflict with John 3:16. Sometimes the word "world" has reference to people and sometimes to worldly things.

V. Lovers of preeminence

   A. Some desire to be above others.

   B. Trying to be first has caused problems among God's people.

   C. 3 John 9

VI. Lovers of darkness

   A. Darkness is opposed to light.

   B. Men of God are of the light and are urged to walk therein (1 John 1:7).

   C. John 3:19-20

VII. Lovers of parents more than of God

    A. Some do not obey the gospel for this reason.

    B. Matthew 10:37

    C. Children are to love their parents, but this must not interfere with their love for God and His word.

    D. Luke 14:26; Mark 10:29-30

Conclusion

I. You can see from these lessons that the Bible has much to say about lovers.

II. Do you love God enough to obey him? Come right now as we sing.

~ 29 ~
Some Needs of the Church

Introduction

I.   From a divine standpoint, the church has no needs.

    A. The church is all-sufficient.

    B. We are complete in Christ (Colossians 2:10).

II.   The church has a human side.

    A. This is where the needs are.

    B. Let's take a look at some of these needs.

Discussion

I.   The church needs preaching preachers.

    A. 2 Timothy 4:1-4

    B. Acts 20:26-27

    C. Titus 2:1

    D. Titus 2:15

        1. Study verses 1-15.

        2. These are things to speak.

    E. Compromise is the order of the day, but we need preaching preachers who preach it just like it is.

II.   The church needs overseeing elders.

103

    A. Many elders fail to see this much-needed work.

    B. Acts 20:28

    C. 1 Peter 5:2-3

        1. This oversight is limited to the "flock of God among you."

        2. This is an ever-continuing job.

    D. Elders will give an account for their work (Hebrews 13:17).

III.   The church needs serving deacons.

    A. 1 Timothy 3:8-13

    B. The work of deacons can be seen in the word "deacon."

        1. A deacon is a servant.

        2. A deacon is like a minute-man—on the job 24 hours a day, serving the church.

        3. A deacon says, "I don't want to be on the job 24 hours a day." Don't be a deacon then!

IV.   The church needs teaching teachers.

    A. One of the great needs of the church today is that of teaching teachers.

    B. Hebrews 5:12

    C. We need teachers who are "faithful and able" (2 Timothy 2:2).

    D. We need dedicated men and women who work at their teaching.

    E. We have in our hands the most precious substance— boys and girls who will be the church of tomorrow.

V.   The church needs working members.

A. The key to church growth is a working membership.

B. God has charged each member with the responsibility of working.

   1. 1 Corinthians 15:58

   2. Philippians 2:12

   3. John 9:4

C. Personal evangelism is necessary if we expect to grow.

   1. 1 Timothy 2:2

   2. 1 Timothy 4:16

D. We are saved to save and are taught to teach.

Conclusion

I.   Summarize these five points.

II. Come join with us in meeting these needs.

~ 30 ~
Running Life's Race
Romans 12:1-2

Introduction

I.   The Bible compares life to many different things. In this lesson it is compared to the running of a race.

II.   Illustration: Suppose a man has a race track and boys are to meet certain requirements in order to enter the race and must run on a certain track. One boy does not enter properly and runs on the outside of the track. Do you think he would be eligible for the prize?

Discussion

I.   All are invited to run in life's race.

    A. Matthew 28:18-29

    B. Mark 16:15-16

    C. Matthew 11:28-30

    D. Revelation 22:17

    E. There are some things all are not invited to.

II.   Must actually enter the race

    A. It is not enough to just hear about it.

    B. Conditions must be met to enter.

       1. Hear, believe, repent, confess, be baptized

2. Lay aside some things (Colossians 3:9)

III. Must then run

   A. Some just sit down on the track.

      1. Hurt self

      2. Hinder others

   B. Philip ran (Acts 8:30).

      1. Ever run in doing the Lord's work?

      2. Ecclesiastes 9:5; 1 Corinthians 15:58

   C. Zeal needed

      1. Titus 2:14

      2. 2 Corinthians 9:2

IV. Must run on the inside of the proper enclosure

   A. Remember the illustration of the boy running on the outside?

   B. A good friend of mine, Bob Underwood, wired a wrong house one time. He got no pay for it as he worked in the wrong place!

   C. The only place we can run life's race and expect to receive the prize is in the church of the Lord.

      1. Acts 20:28

      2. Do you think God would send His only Son, and He would give His life to purchase the church, and give us a prize for not being in it?

      3. Acts 2:47

      4. Ephesians 5:23

V. Must run with patience

   A. Hebrews 6:12

    B. Hebrews 12:1-2

    C. James 5:7

    D. We are living in an impatient world.

    E. We must preserve.

VI.   Run with your eyes on the Lord.

    A. "Looking unto Jesus" (Hebrews 12:2)

    B. Need to look to Jesus for

       1. An example (1 Peter 2:21)

       2. Strength (Philippians 4:13)

VII. Must abide by the rules

    A. 2 Timothy 2:5

       1. The New American Standard Version says, "And also, if anyone competes as an athlete, he does not win the prize unless he competes according to the rules."

       2. This is the idea also of "striving lawfully!"

    B. Philippians 3:15

    C. Some act as if we had no rules. The word of God is the rule book. It must be followed.

VIII. Must run until the race is over

    A. If you drop out, you will be disqualified.

    B. Galatians 5:7; 1 Timothy 6:12; Luke 9:62

    C. Can be reinstated by repentance, confession and prayer.

       1. Acts 8:13-22

       2. 1 John 1:9

IX.   Christ to judge the race

    A. John 5:22; Romans 2:16

    B. By the rule book (John 12:48)

    C. Individually by how we have run (Romans 14:12; 2 Corinthians 5:10)

X.   A prize at the end of the race

    A. 1 Corinthians 9:24-27

    B. Philippians 2:16

    C. Philippians 3:14

    D. 1 Peter 1:3-4

    E. 2 Timothy 4:6-8

Conclusion

I.   Have you entered the race?

II.   If not, why not now?

~ 31 ~
Possessing the Mind of Christ
Philippians 2:5-8

Introduction

I.   Christians must be like Christ.

II.   Read and discuss.

    A. Romans 8:9

    B. 1 Corinthians 2:16

    C. Romans 8:10

Discussion

I.   Mind of humility

    A. Philippians 2:5-8

    B. Matthew 20:28

    C. Proverbs 18:12

    D. 1 Peter 3:4; 1 Peter 5:5-6

    E. Paul served with humility (Acts 10:19).

II.   Unselfish mind

    A. Christ gave all (2 Corinthians 8:9).

    B. Luke 14:33

    C. Christ did not please himself (Romans 15:3).

  D. Acts 26:23

III. Mind of tenderness and love

  A. Every act of Christ was motivated by love for man and His Father.

  B. John 15:13

  C. Ephesians 5:1-2

  D. 1 Corinthians 15:3

  E. Ephesians 5:25

IV. Mind to work

  A. Jesus worked (John 9:4; John 17:4).

  B. John 20:30-31; John 21:25

  C. Nehemiah 4:6

  D. We must work (1 Corinthians 15:58).

V. Forgiving mind

  A. Luke 23:34

  B. 2 Corinthians 2:7

  C. Colossians 3:13

  D. God forgives only as we practice forgiveness.

VI. Mind of unity—one mind

  A. God and Jesus were united.

   1. John 17:20-21

   2. Jesus came to do the will of His Father.

  B. We must be united.

   1. 1 Corinthians 1:10

   2. Romans 12:16

      3. Must be of the same mind in the Lord (Philippians 4:2)

      4. 1 Peter 3:8

      5. 1 Peter 4:1

VII. Sacrificial mind

    A. Jesus gave his own life for man.

    B. Philippians 2:5-8

    C. Hebrews 2:9

    D. Hebrews 7:27

    E. We must make some sacrifice (Romans 12:1-2).

VIII. An obedient mind

    A. Jesus was obedient (Philippians 2:5-8).

    B. Hebrews 5:8-9

    C. We must obey.

      1. Matthew 7:21

      2. Luke 6:46

      3. Revelation 22:14

Conclusion

I.   Do you have the mind of Christ?

II.   Have you obeyed God and made your life right with God? If not, come right now as we stand to sing.

~ 32 ~
Putting Christ Back In

Introduction

I.   Around December 25, we hear the expression concerning "putting Christ back in Christmas."

    A. An impossibility, for He was never in it

    B. The date of his birth is unknown as to the month.

II.   Let's use the expression to learn some other lessons.

Discussion

I.   Christ needs to be put back in the position of authority.

    A. Matthew 28:18

    B. Matthew 7:29

    C. John 7:46

    D. John 2:5

    E. Matthew 17:5

II.   Put back in as God's spokesman

    A. The only way that God speaks to man today is by His Son.

        1. Hebrews 1:1-2

        2. Matthew 17:5

B. Thus, we need to listen to him.

III. As the savior of the world

   A. Matthew 1:21; Luke 2:11; 1 Timothy 1:15

   B. Hebrews 5:8-9; Luke 19:10

   C. Many have removed Him from the place of being savior.

   D. We must respect and teach His plan for saving man.

      1. Hearing, believing, repenting, confessing and being baptized (Matthew 17:5; John 8:24; Acts 17:30; Matthew 10:32; Mark 16:16)

      2. Remaining faithful and steadfast (1 Corinthians 15:58)

IV. Back in the church as head

   A. Ephesians 1:22-23; Colossians 1:18

   B. Source of many problems by not recognizing his headship

   C. The body can only do as the head directs (Ephesians 5:23).

V. Back in our homes

   A. Fathers, mothers, boys and girls must each learn their place in the home and get in it—then stay there.

   B. Ephesians 6:1-4; Ephesians 5:22-31

VI. We need to put Christ back in Christians.

   A. Philippians 3:16

   B. Hebrews 2:10

   C. Galatians 2:20

   D. 2 Peter 3:11

   E. 2 Corinthians 3:2

F. We need to let the world see Christ living in us.

VII. Put Christ back in the name we wear.

A. The word Christian contains the name of Christ.

B. This is the name we need to wear.

1. Acts 11:26

2. Acts 26:28

3. 1 Peter 4:16

VIII. Christ needs to be put back in our preaching.

A. The theme of New Testament preaching was that of Christ.

B. Acts 8:5, 12

C. Acts 8:35

D. 1 Corinthians 2:1-2

E. 2 Corinthians 4:5

F. 2 Timothy 4:1-4

G. Today, about everything else is preached.

1. Puppet shows

2. Book reviews

3. Social gospel

Conclusion

I. After all, "putting Christ back in" is not a bad idea, provided we put him back in the right things.

II. Have you put Christ in your life? If not, come right now as we sing.

~ 33 ~
The Need for Some Changes

Introduction

I.   The Bible teaches the need for men to make changes.

II.   Repentance means to change

    A. Acts 2:38

    B. Acts 3:19

    C. Acts 17:30

    D. 2 Peter 3:9

    E. Repentance is not just for the alien sinner.

Discussion

I.   From a lack of reverence to really worshipping God

    A. One of the many great blessings of God's people is that of worship.

    B. Yet many do not really worship God.

    C. Two elements of acceptable worship

        1. In spirit and in truth

        2. John 4:24

    D. The wrong object

        1. The devil (Matthew 4:8-10)

2. Men (Acts 10:25-26)

3. Angels (Revelation 22:8-9)

E. The right object

    1. God

    2. Matthew 4:10; Revelation 22:9

    3. When we have the wrong object, we need to make a change.

II. A change from the services being a weariness to gladness

A. Malachi 1:6-13

    1. The priests of the Old Testament despised their duty here and had no heart in it.

    2. It was a weariness—just a burden.

B. Do you ever say, "Well, we have to go to church again"?

C. Psalms 122:1

D. 2 Corinthians 8:12

E. Need to cultivate an appetite for spiritual things (1 Peter 2:1-2; Matthew 5:6; 1 Peter 2:5)

III. A change from ignorance to knowledge

A. There is a great demand for those who know.

B. The Lord has always demanded that His people know.

    1. Hosea 4:6

    2. Deuteronomy 5:1

    3. 2 Peter 3:18

    4. Matthew 9:13

    5. Matthew 11:29

    6. 2 Timothy 2:15

       7. 1 Timothy 4:13

       8. Revelation 1:3

IV.   From infancy to maturity

    A. There are too many grown babies in most churches.

       1. Pout

       2. Won't speak to each other

       3. Need to grow up

    B. 1 Corinthians 14:20

    C. 1 Corinthians 16:13

       1. To quit means to behave like a man

       2. Grow up

    D. Ephesians 4:14

    E. I heard of a group that couldn't agree on a roof for a church building. Some wanted shingles, while others wanted tin. They decided to shingle half of the building and put tin on the other half. Those who wanted shingles sat under the shingle side, and those who wanted tin sat under the tin side! Don't you think these need to grow up?

V.   From laziness to zeal

    A. There is entirely too much laziness and lack of concern on the part of many.

    B. Amos 6:1

    C. Ecclesiastes 9:10

    D. Lamentations 1:12

    E. 2 Corinthians 7:11; 9:2

    F. Titus 2:14

  G. No wonder churches grow so little.

VI. From minimums to maximums

  A. Not how little but how much

  B. Suppose God had thought in terms of how little I can do for man. These passages would not have been in the Bible:

   1. John 3:16

   2. Romans 5:8

   3. 2 Corinthians 8:9

  C. Luke 17:20

Conclusion

I. If you are here and never obeyed the gospel, you need to change.

  A. Your mind in repentance (Acts 17:30)

  B. Your relationship in baptism (Galatians 3:27)

  C. Come hearing, believing, and obeying

II. If you have left the fold, make the necessary changes as we sing.

~ 34 ~

Pleasing God

1 Corinthians 10:5

Introduction

I.   Our greatest desire should be to please God.

II.   God is not pleased with just anything.

Discussion

I.   Must strive to please God

    A. 2 Timothy 2:4

    B. Colossians 1:10

    C. Hebrews 12:21

    D. 1 John 3:22

    E. Hebrews 11:5

    F. Proverbs 16:7

    G. 1 Thessalonians 4:1

II.   Must not try to please self

    A. Romans 15:1-2

    B. Colossians 2:23

III.   Christ did not please himself.

    A. Romans 15:3

    B. Matthew 26:39

IV. Cannot please men

    A. Galatians 1:10

    B. Some try it (2 Timothy 4:1-4)

V. Some things God is pleased with

    A. The life of His Son, Jesus

       1. Matthew 3:17

       2. Matthew 17:5

    B. The death of His Son

       1. Isaiah 53:1-10

       2. 1 Peter 2:21-25

    C. Praising the name of God with song

       1. Psalms 69:30-31

       2. Ephesians 5:19

       3. Colossians 3:16

       4. Hebrews 13:15

       5. Hebrews 2:12

    D. To make Israel His people

       1. 1 Samuel 12:22

       2. Christians today are the Israel of God (Romans 2:28-29).

    E. The resurrected new body

       1. 1 Corinthians 15:25-28

       2. Philippians 3:21; 1 John 3:2

    F. The life of Enoch

       1. Hebrews 11:5

       2. Genesis 5:21-24

G. When children obey their parents

    1. Colossians 3:20

    2. Ephesians 6:1-4

    3. Proverbs 22:6

    4. Takes effort to bring this about

H. Spiritual sacrifices

    1. Hebrews 13:15-16

    2. Romans 12:1-2

    3. Philippians 4:15-18

    4. 1 Peter 2:5

I. That all fulness dwells in Jesus

    1. Colossians 1:16-19

    2. Colossians 2:9-10

J. Setting the members in the body

    1. 1 Corinthians 12:18

    2. Context: 1 Corinthians 12:14-27

    3. Spiritual gifts: Each had only one gift and thus had to work together.

K. Through the foolishness of preaching to save the believer

    1. 1 Corinthians 1:21

    2. 1 Corinthians 1:17; 2:5

Conclusion

I. Hebrews 11:6

II. Come now.

~ 35 ~
The Christian and Evangelism
2 Timothy 2:2

Introduction

I.   The Bible teaches personal evangelism.

    A. John 1:40-41

    B. 2 Timothy 2:2

    C. 1 Timothy 4:6; Acts 20:20

    D. Acts 8:4; Acts 5:42; Hebrews 5:12

II.   The religion of Jesus Christ is a teaching religion.

    A. John 6:44-45

    B. Matthew 28:18-20

    C. Mark 16:15-16

Discussion

I.   Requirements of doing personal evangelism: preparation

    A. Ezra 7:10

        1. Preparation—obey yourself (Romans 2:21-22; 2 Corinthians 8:5), then teach and practice what you preach.

        2. Need to be overflowing with the word (2 Corinthians 3:2)!

    B. Proper attitude (Galatians 6:1; Romans 15:1; Matthew 5:16; Philippians 2:15)

II.   "The fruit of the righteous is a tree of life; and he that winneth souls is wise" (Proverbs 11:30).

    A. Mark 1:17

III.   Let's take the word "evangelism" and, for each letter, suggest a word.

    A. *E—Endurance*

       1. We need to understand when we do personal evangelism that we must have endurance. Not everyone we try to teach will listen. Not every one will be reached. Remember the parable of the sower (Luke 8).

       2. In the selling field, 80 percent of the sales are made after the fifth call! The Los Angeles Executive Club said 48 percent make one call and quit; 25 percent make two calls and quit. 2 Peter 3:15—longsuffering.

    B. *V—Value of a soul*

       1. Eternal (2 Corinthians 5:1)

       2. Made in God's image (Genesis 1:26-27)

       3. Value of just one soul (Matthew 16:26)

       4. Jesus spent much time in just teaching one soul. Only 16 discourses were of a public nature—the rest, personal.

          a. Woman at the well (John 4)

          b. Zaccheus (Luke 19:5)

          c. Nicodemus (John 3)

       5. An *infidel's* statement about the value of the soul

(Gatewood on Personal Work—p. 66)

C. *A—Able*

1. Your responsibility is determined, in part, by your ability (2 Timothy 2:2).

2. Talents (Matthew 25:14-30)

3. 1 Peter 3:15

4. Romans 15:14

5. Colossians 4:6

D. *N—Now is the time to begin.*

1. Too often we intend to do personal evangelism. If we are not careful, we will be in the class of those of whom Jesus said, "...for they say and do not" (Matthew 23:3).

2. Must do it (Matthew 7:21; Luke 6:46)

3. John 9:4; John 4:35; Matthew 9:37-38

E. *G—Gospel must be taught* (Romans 1:16).

1. Matthew 28:18-20; Mark 16:15-16

2. Use the scriptures (1 Corinthians 15:1-8; Acts 14:7)

F. *E—Enthusiasm*

1. "...Philip ran..." (Acts 8:30)

2. Need to be zealous (Titus 2:14)

3. A salesman must know his product and be sold on it.

4. Must be friendly (Proverbs 18:24)

G. *L—Love for lost souls*

1. Mark 12:31

2. Romans 10:1; Romans 9:3; 1 Thessalonians 2:8

3. 2 Corinthians 12:15—If we expect the lost to be concerned about what we teach, we must be concerned about the lost (John 3:16; Romans 5:8)!

H. *I—Individual responsibility*

1. Not very often does the individual Christian realize that he has any responsibility toward evangelism except helping support the preacher by his Lord's day contribution!

2. Must warn the wicked (Galatians 6:1; Ezekiel 3:18-19; 2 Timothy 2:2; Acts 20:26-27; Acts 20:30)

3. Acts 5:42

4. Acts 8:4-5

5. Philippians 1:14

6. Philippians 2:15-16; John 1:40-41

7. Repeat the story 30 times!

I. *S—Salvation the result*

1. 1 Timothy 4:16; James 5:19-20

2. Men are in sin, no hope, wages is death (Romans 3:23; Ephesians 2:12; Romans 6:23)

3. Illustration: There is a million dollars, but before you can have it, you must help another get some too!

J. *M—Minister: Every Christian is one*

1. A minister is a servant.

2. We need to get away from the idea that the preacher is "*the* minister." "...By love serve one another" (Galatians 5:13; Mark 10:43-45).

Conclusion

I.   We must obey the word, then be enthusiastic in doing all of it.

II.   Come today and be a child of God.

~ 36 ~
Go and Learn

Introduction

I.   Teaching has ever had an important place in God's dealings with man (Deuteronomy 4:14; Deuteronomy 6:6-7). Israel was told to teach their children. The prophets of old taught the "good and right way" (1 Samuel 12:23).

II. Jesus was a great teacher.

   A. John 3:2; Matthew 4:23

   B. Sent out the 12 and 70 to teach (Matthew 28:19; Acts 5:42; 2 Timothy 4:2). When the Bible emphasizes the need for teaching, it also teaches the importance of *learning*. Actually, no teaching takes place unless there is learning. Learning is to gain knowledge or understanding of, or skill in, by study, instruction or investigation.

Discussion

I.   Learning is important.

   A. Matthew 11:28-30

   B. Matthew 9:13

   C. John 6:44-45

   D. Many things God wants us to learn (Matthew 24:32)

II.   Some things we must learn

   A. Learn to fear God.

      1. Deuteronomy 4:10

      2. Ecclesiastes 12:13-14

      3. Fear of God required to please Him

         a. Acts 10:34-35

         b. Acts 10:2

         c. Deuteronomy 31:13

         d. Deuteronomy 17:19

   B. Learn God's statutes.

      1. Psalms 119:71

      2. Often time, afflictions can cause us to learn some valuable lessons (Deuteronomy 5:1).

      3. Statutes—an established rule or law

   C. We need to learn God's law.

      1. Galatians 6:2

      2. Psalms 119:73

   D. Learn of Christ.

      1. That he is the Savior (Matthew 11:29)

      2. Luke 19:10

      3. Mediator (2 Timothy 2:5)

      4. Has all authority (Matthew 28:18)

      5. Heads the church (Ephesians 1:22-23)

      6. Judge (John 5:22)

   E. Learn to do well.

    1. Isaiah 1:17

    2. Too many have "just get by" attitude

    3. Worth doing is worth doing right (Ecclesiastes 9:10)!

F. Learn contentment.

    1. Hebrews 13:5

    2. Philippians 4:11

G. Learn doctrine.

    1. Isaiah 29:24

    2. Acts 2:42; 2 John 9; 1 Timothy 4:16

H. Learn righteousness.

    1. Isaiah 26:9

    2. Psalms 119:172

    3. Acts 10:34-35

I. Learn to maintain good works.

    1. Titus 3:14

    2. The responsibility of every individual Christian

    3. Matthew 5:14-16

J. Learn to care for needy relatives so the church will not be burdened.

    1. 1 Timothy 5:4, 16

    2. Learn by being taught.

K. Learn not to think of men above that which is written.

    1. 1 Corinthians 4:6

    2. Romans 12:3; Galatians 6:3

L. Learn to abide in divine revelation.

1. 2 John 9

2. 2 Timothy 3:16-17

3. 1 Peter 4:11

4. Galatians 1:11-12

M. God demands mercy, not sacrifice.

1. Matthew 9:13 (a quote from Hosea 6:6)

2. 2 Timothy 3:7; 1 Timothy 2:3-4

III.   Some things not to learn

A. To do after the abominations of other nations (Deuteronomy 18:9-12)

B. The ways of an angry, furious man (Proverbs 22:24-25)

C. War (Isaiah 2:4; Micah 4:3)

D. Way of the heathen (Jeremiah 10:2)

E. To be idle (1 Timothy 5:13)

Conclusion

I.   We have seen the importance of learning, some things we must learn, and some things we must not learn.

II.   Now would you learn the importance of obedience by coming, believing, repenting, confessing and being baptized right now as we sing.

~ 37 ~
Selecting a Church
Matthew 16:13-20

Introduction

I.   There comes a time in all or our lives when we have to make a decision.

    A. Where to go to school

    B. Whom to marry

    C. Life's work

    D. What church to be a member of

II.   Some think so little about selecting a church.

Discussion

I.   How not to select a church

    A. The nearest one

        1. Do not choose a church "just because it's around the corner."

        2. The closest one may not be the right one.

        3. We go great distances for other things.

            a. Finding a good doctor

            b. Buying a car

            c. Shopping for clothes

d. To work

B. One with an impressive building

   1. Elaborate and costly building do attract people.

   2. The meeting house does not determine the quality of the teaching.

   3. The church is not the building (Acts 5:11).

C. Because friends and relatives attend

   1. Friendship does not determine truth.

   2. Must love the Lord above friends and relatives (Matthew 10:37)

D. Not because it has a large membership

   1. "This many people can't be wrong" attitude

   2. Size of a church doesn't make it right

   3. Only eight saved in the ark (1 Peter 3:20)

   4. Matthew 7:13-14

   5. Just because a lot of people think it's right doesn't make it right (Isaiah 55:8-9; Proverbs 14:12).

E. Not because of the social activities provided

   1. Recreation and entertainment used by some to attract people to come

   2. Such is not the work of the church (Romans 14:17)

   3. Reward motivations are used by many in the "bus ministry."

II. Guidelines for selecting a church

A. One that respects the authority of the Bible

   1. Idea exists that it doesn't matter too much about what the Bible says

2. The word of God must determine what we do in religion.

3. 2 Timothy 2:16-17; 2 Peter 1:3; Matthew 28:18

B. One that is identified as belonging to Christ

1. Acts 8:1-3

2. Matthew 16:18

3. Romans 16:16

4. The church belongs to Christ.

C. One in which its members wear a Bible name

1. There is something in a name.

2. God named His people (Isaiah 62:2; Isaiah 56:5; Isaiah 65:15).

3. Acts 11:26; Acts 26:28; 1 Peter 4:16

4. There is no authority for wearing human names.

D. One that worships like the New Testament teaches

1. The Lord's church engaged in teaching, fellowship, the Lord's supper every week, praying and singing.

2. Acts 2:42; 1 Corinthians 16:1-2; Acts 20:7; Ephesians 5:19; Colossians 3:16

3. John 4:24

4. We must make sure that our worship is not in vain (Matthew 15:9).

E. One organized after the New Testament order

1. Elders, deacons, and members

a. Acts 14:23

b. Philippians 1:1

2. With Christ as head (Colossians 1:18)

3. No larger nor smaller organization than the local church

F. One satisfied to just be the church and do the work God assigned her

   1. Too many churches want to engage in things for which there is no authority.

   2. Many are spending money on schemes and projects which cannot be read about in the Bible.

   3. The work of the church is spiritual.

      a. Preaching the gospel (1 Thessalonians 1:8; 1 Timothy 3:15; Philippians 4:15-16; 2 Corinthians 11:8)

      b. Taking care of its own needy (Acts 6:1-6; Acts 11:27-30; 1 Timothy 5:16)

      c. Providing a place to worship (Hebrews 10:25; 1 Corinthians 14:23)

   4. There leaves no place for the church sending money to the college, sponsoring churches, and societies started by men.

G. One that teaches the Bible plan of salvation

   1. Hear, believe, repent, confess Christ, be baptized, live faithfully

   2. Matthew 17:5; John 8:2-4; Acts 17:30; Matthew 10:32; Mark 16:16; Revelation 2:10

Conclusion

I. If you would be a member of the right church, then select to obey right now.

II. The Lord will add you to His church (Acts 2:47).

~ 38 ~
Which of the Two?
Joshua 24:15; 1 Kings 18:21

Introduction

I.   God made man a free moral agent; he can choose to obey or reject God.

II.   Thus, there are two.

Discussion

I.   There are two gates.

A. Narrow and broad gate (Matthew 7:13-14)

B. Strait means narrow, compressed.

C. Enter: cannot enter as we are—sin

1. Lay aside old man of sin (Colossians 3:5-19; Hebrews 12:1-2)

2. Cease to be self-willed (Matthew 16:24)

3. Discard things of this world (1 Corinthians 6:9-11), repentance (Acts 17:30)

D. Broad gate

1. Large for man to enter without laying aside his cargo of sin

2. Does not have to make a single change in his life

II. Two ways

   A. Refers to the walks of life

   B. Must come through the narrow gate to walk in the
       narrow way

   C. To walk in the light (1 John 1:7; John 14:6)

   D. Two ways

      1. Broad and narrow

      2. Broad way allows man to do as he pleases; narrow
          restricts.

III. Two groups

   A. The few

      1. Broad and narrow

      2. God's people have always been in the minority
          (1 Peter 3:20-21; Deuteronomy 7:7); fewest of all
          people

   B. The many

      1. Broad way is traveled by the many, no resistance.

      2. The easy way, popular way

IV. Two destinies

   A. Two gates lead to two ways, traveling toward two
       destinies.

   B. Narrow way leads to life

      1. 1 John 5:11; Romans 6:22

      2. 1 Timothy 6:12; Deuteronomy 30:15, 20

   C. Broad way leads to destruction (Joshua 21:8)

      1. 2 Thessalonians 1:7-9

2. Destruction means the loss of eternal life.

Conclusion

I.   Since there are two, now you must decide.

II.   Come as we sing.

~ 39 ~

The Worship of the New Testament Church

Introduction

I. The history of man reveals that man is sure to worship the object of his devotion.

II. The New Testament reveals the worship of the church.

Discussion

I. Five kinds of worship in the Bible

   A. Vain worship

      1. Matthew 15:9

      2. Vain means to no avail or to no profit. Do these worship? Yes, but in vain,

   B. Ignorant worship

      1. Acts 17:23

   C. Will worship

      1. Colossians 2:23

   D. Mock worship

      1. Mark 15:19-20

  E. True worship

    1. John 4:14

II. Two elements of acceptable worship

  A. John 4:24

    1. In spirit—right disposition

    2. In truth (John 17:17)—according to the truth of God

  B. 1 Peter 2:5

III. The object of man's worship

  A. Must not be

    1. Men (Acts 10:25-26)

    2. Devil (Matthew 4:10)

    3. Angels (Revelation 22:8-9)

  B. Object must be God

    1. Matthew 4:10

    2. John 4:24

    3. Revelation 22:9

IV. Avenues of worship

  A. Prayer

    1. Acts 2:42

    2. Conditions of prayer

      a. In the name of Christ (John 14:14)

      b. In faith (James 1:6)

      c. Worshipper of God (John 9:31)

      d. Doer of will (John 9:31)

      e. According to will (1 John 5:14)

    3. Christ the Mediator (1 Timothy 2:5)

B. Apostles doctrine (Acts 2:42)

    1. Teachings (2 John 9; 1 Timothy 1:3)

    2. Matthew 28:19

C. Fellowship (giving)

    1. 1 Corinthians 16:1-2

    2. 2 Corinthians 9:6-7

    3. Luke 6:38

    4. No authority to raise money by selling suppers, being in business, and the like.

    5. Money used for

        a. Supporting preachers (2 Corinthians 11:8; Philippians 4:16-17)

        b. Assisting needy saints (Acts 6; Acts 11:27-30; 1 Timothy 5:16)

D. Breaking of bread (Lord's supper)

    1. Acts 20:7; 1 Corinthians 11:23-34

    2. Two elements: bread and fruit of the vine

        a. Unleavened bread (Exodus 12:15)

        b. Body and blood to be remembered

E. Vocal music

    1. Matthew 26:30; Mark 14:26; Acts 16:25; Romans 15:9; 1 Corinthians 14:15; Ephesians 5:19; Colossians 3:16; Hebrews 2:12; Hebrews 13:15; James 5:13)

      2. Mechanical music not authorized in the New Testament worship

V.   Four requirements

    A. God chose the place (Deuteronomy 16:2).

      1. Jerusalem

      2. The church (Ephesians 3:21)

    B. God told them what to do.

      1. Deuteronomy 16:16

      2. Can only do as told

    C. Told them what not to do

      1. Deuteronomy 16:21-22

      2. Must respect God's word

    D. Told them how to do it

      1. Deuteronomy 16:11

      2. We need to rejoice (Philippians 3:3)

Conclusion

I.   We must worship as God directs in order to please Him.

II.   Come now to obey as we sing.

~ 40 ~
Some Things Everyone Needs to Know

Introduction

I.   There are some things in life man can get by without knowing.

II.   I would like to call to our attention some things we must all know.

Discussion

I.   There is a God.

   A. Genesis 1:1

   B. Exodus 20:3

   C. Psalms 19:1

   D. Acts 17:28

      1. Goodness and severity

      2. Romans 11:22

II.   The Bible is the word of God.

   A. 2 Timothy 3:16-17; 2 Peter 1:21

   B. 2 Peter 1:3

   C. 1 Thessalonians 2:13

III.   The word of God must not be changed, but we must abide in it.

    A. Deuteronomy 4:2

    B. Proverbs 30:6

    C. 1 Corinthians 4:6

    D. 2 John 9; Revelation 22:18-19

    E. Galatians 1:6-9

IV.   Man today lives under law to Christ.

    A. Galatians 6:2; Galatians 2:21; Hebrews 10:9

    B. Hebrews 9:16-17; Romans 6:14

    C. He has all authority (Matthew 7:29; Matthew 28:18).

V.   Because of sin, Christ died to become man's Savior.

    A. Sin means to miss the mark (Romans 3:23; 1 John 3:4).

    B. Matthew 1:21; Luke 2:11; Romans 5:8

    C. Luke 19:10; 1 Timothy 1:15

VI.   Man has the responsibility of obeying God.

    A. Ecclesiastes 12:13-14; Matthew 7:21

    B. Luke 6:46; Romans 6:17-18; Hebrews 5:8

    C. Revelation 22:14

VII. Jesus died to establish His church for men to be in and worship.

    A. Matthew 16:18

    B. Purchased (Acts 20:28); head (Colossians 1:18); Savior (Ephesians 5:23)

    C. Worship in (John 4:24)

VIII. God still demands righteous living.

    A. Titus 2:11-12

    B. 1 Timothy 5:22

    C. Ephesians 4:28-32

    D. Romans 12

IX. Man must make preparation for death.

    A. Amos 4:12

    B. How? While he lives.

X. Man will be judged by how he lives.

    A. Romans 14:12

    B. By the word (John 12:48)

Conclusion

I. We know by the things that we have heard today, we must obey His word.

II. Why not come and obey Him now?

~ 41 ~

What God Hath Joined Together

Matthew 19:3-9

Introduction

I. God has joined a number of things together.

II. We must not separate what God joins together.

Discussion

I. God joins husband and wife.

    A. Matthew 19:4-6

    B. God is the author of marriage.

        1. He joined the first pair.

        2. Genesis 2:18-24

    C. Marriage is a sacred relationship and is holy.

        1. God joined

        2. Hebrews 13:4

    D. Marriage is to be permanent.

        1. It is a life-long affair.

        2. Romans 7:1-4

    E. Death and fornication only can break the marriage bond.

        1. Romans 7:1-4

  2. Matthew 19:9

II. Christ and the church

  A. Some would say, "Take Christ and forget about the church."

    1. Cannot be done

    2. Go together

  B. The church is the body of Christ.

    1. Ephesians 5:22-32

    2. Ephesians 1:22-23; Colossians 1:18

    3. The only way you could separate me from my physical body is to kill me (James 2:26).

  C. To oppose the church is to oppose Christ.

    1. Saul persecuted the church (Acts 8:1).

    2. In so doing, he persecuted Christ (Acts 9:4).

III. Worship in spirit and in truth

  A. Can't worship any old way

  B. God has joined spirit and truth.

    1. John 4:24

    2. We must worship in the right attitude and according to the truth.

    3. You cannot have one without the other and please God.

IV. Works and faith

  A. Many take the faith and leave off the works.

  B. God has joined works and faith.

    1. James 2:14-26

       2. Faith is only known through our works.

   C. The faith that saves is the faith that works.

       1. Galatians 5:6

       2. Acts 10:34-35

V.   Sin and death

   A. Sin by that name is disappearing.

       1. A thing to many is no longer a sin but a disease.

       2. Sin is still sin (Romans 3:23; 1 John 3:4).

   B. The consequences of sin is death.

       1. Ezekiel 18:4

       2. Romans 6:23

       3. James 1:14-15

   C. You will not separate sin and death.

VI.   Belief and baptism

   A. Many want to separate

   B. Mark 16:16

   C. The Lord tied these together for salvation.

       1. Cannot be saved by belief before baptism

       2. Saul was baptized because he believed (Acts 9:6; Acts 22:16)

VII. Unbelief and damnation

   A. Mark 16:16

   B. Many think that baptism is not essential.

       1. Because of the phrase, "but he that believeth not shall be damned" (Mark 16:16).

       2. Really, the Lord is joining unbelief and damnation.

C. John 3:18

D. The unbeliever will be lost (Revelation 21:8).

Conclusion

I.   We must not separate what God joins together.

II.   Come right now, believing and obeying, as we sing.

~ 42 ~

How Some People Read the Bible

Luke 10:25-29

Introduction

I. Jesus drove home the point as He asked the lawyer, "What is written in the law? How readest thou?"

II. The Bible is to be read and understood.

    A. 2 Timothy 2:15

    B. 1 Timothy 4:13

    C. Colossians 4:16

    D. Let's ask how some people read the Bible on various subjects.

Discussion

I. How readest thou about the church?

    A. Some read it, "I will build Martin Luther's church."

    B. But Jesus said, "I will build my church" (Matthew 16:18).

    C. Some think they read that the church is not important.

        1. The saved are added to it (Acts 2:47).

        2. Christ is the Savior of it (Ephesians 5:23-25).

    D. Some read that there are many churches.

1. The Bible teaches there is only one.

2. There is one body and the body is the church (Ephesians 4:4; Colossians 1:18).

II. How readest thou about baptism?

   A. Some read it, "Baptism doth also *not* save us."

   B. Peter said that baptism saves (1 Peter 3:21).

   C. Jesus said it is essential (Mark 16:16).

   D. Peter said it was for the remission of sins (Acts 2:38).

   E. How readest thou?

III. How readest thou about faith?

   A. Some read that salvation is by faith only.

   B. James says it is not by faith only (James 2:24-26).

   C. Nothing alone is ever said to save.

   D. Faith must be put to work in obedience.

      1. Galatians 5:6

      2. Acts 10:34-35

IV. How readest thou about praying?

   A. Some read to pray when in a tight spot.

   B. Paul said to pray without ceasing (1 Thessalonians 5:17).

   C. Acts 2:42

   D. Philippians 4:6

V. How readest thou about falling from grace?

   A. Some read, "Ye are *not* fallen from grace."

   B. Read what Paul told the Galatians (Galatians 5:4).

   C. 1 Corinthians 10:12

    D. 2 Peter 3:17

    E. 2 Peter 2:20-22

VI. How readest thou about raising money?

    A. Paul said to "give as prospered" (1 Corinthians 16:2).

    B. Some read that any way is ok, such as sales—the church being in some kind of business and the like.

    C. As to members giving, some read it, "Lay by in store what is left over."

    D. Acts 20:35; 2 Corinthians 9:6-7; Luke 6:38

VII. How readest thou about church music?

    A. Some read to sing and play.

    B. The New Testament teaches us to sing.

       1. Matthew 16:30

       2. Mark 14:26

       3. Acts 16:25

       4. Romans 15:9

       5. 1 Corinthians 14:15

       6. Ephesians 5:19

       7. Colossians 3:16

       8. Hebrews 2:12

       9. Hebrews 13:15

       10. James 5:13

    C. Did you hear the word "play" in any of these passages?

VIII. How readest thou about being faithful?

    A. Some read it, "just be baptized and do as I please."

B. The Bible teaches that we must be faithful to be saved eternally.

    1. Matthew 24:13

    2. Revelation 2:10

    3. 1 Corinthians 15:58

Conclusion

I.   How have you been reading the Bible?

II.   Have you read that you are a sinner and need to obey? Come now as we stand and sing.

~ 43 ~
The Silence of the Scriptures

Introduction

I.   Thomas Campbell said in 1808, "Where the Bible speaks, we speak; where the Bible is silent, we are silent." This became the motto of the Restoration Movement.

II.   A much needed principle for today

    A. 1 Peter 4:11

    B. Colossians 3:17

Discussion

I.   The importance of authority

    A. God is over all (Ephesians 4:6; 1 Corinthians 11:3; 1 Corinthians 15:27).

    B. God gave authority to His Son (Matthew 28:18; Ephesians 1:22-23).

    C. Authority established

        1. By a statement of fact (Genesis 1:1)

        2. By a direct command (Acts 2:38)

        3. By approved apostolic examples (Acts 14:23)

        4. By necessary inference (Matthew 3:16)

D. Authority may be general or specific.

1. If general, we must not bind a specific. God gave us the authority for assembling together (Hebrews 10:25), so we have authority for a place to meet. He did not bind the specifics. We may buy, rent or whatever.

2. If specific, we must bind that which is specified, for all other things are excluded.

   a. God specified gopher wood in the building of the ark (Genesis 6:14). Other kinds of wood were excluded.

   b. God specified singing as the kind of music for the Christian in worship (Ephesians 5:19). Even though the Bible does not say *not* to use instrumental music in worship, no man has the God-given right to grant a liberty where God's authority excludes.

   c. In regard to institutionalism, God has specified that the local church do its own work under the elders of that local church (Acts 14:23; Philippians 1:1; 1 Peter 5:2; Acts 20:28). Since God made no other arrangements for the work to be done, the silence of the scriptures must be respected.

E. Two extremes

1. In order for a thing to be scriptural, it must be specifically authorized.

2. For a thing to be wrong, it must be specifically condemned.

3. Both are wrong!

      4. One binds where God has not bound, and one looses where God has bound.

II.   Binding and loosing

    A. All of the apostles were given binding and loosing power.

      1. Matthew 16:19; Matthew 18:18

      2. They were to bind that which had been bound and loose only that which God has loosed.

    B. The word is settled in Heaven (Psalms 119:89).

    C. The apostles could only speak that which was revealed (Galatians 1:11-12; Acts 4:20).

III.   Commandments and no commandments

    A. Acts 15:24

    B. We must respect what God has said and not base our religion on things God has not said.

    C. Nadab and Abihu operated in the realm of no commandments (Leviticus 10:1-2). Remember what happened to them!

IV.   The importance of the silence of the scriptures

    A. God said nothing about an angel being His Son (Hebrews 1:1-2). He was silent on the matter.

    B. God, through Moses, said nothing about priests from the tribe of Judah (Hebrews 7:14).

      1. God did not allow it even though he was silent on it.

      2. Hebrews 8:4; Hebrews 7:12; Hebrews 4:15

    C. Silence on a Bible subject does not give one the right to assume (Deuteronomy 18:20; Psalms 19:13; 2 Peter 2:10; Numbers 15:30).

D. Illustrate

    1. The retail market: Suppose that I order a pair of shoes—size 8 1/2, color blue, D width. I believe that this excludes every other color, size and width. My silence is important. If silence means nothing, I might get a deep-freeze along with my shoes! Right?

V. Doesn't say not to

    A. The old argument is used to try to justify instrumental music and many other things. People argue that if the Bible does not tell us *not* to do a thing, then we can do it. This kind of thinking would justify ham and gravy on the Lord's table. If not, why not?

VI. Consequences of the doctrine

    A. Opens the floodgate to every innovation known to man

    B. Would bring into the worship acts without faith

    C. Ignores God's law of exclusion

VII. Some applications

    A. Some things the Bible is silent on

        1. Instrumental music in worship

        2. Sprinkling or pouring for baptism

        3. Lent observance

        4. Easter

    B. 1 Peter 4:11

Conclusion

I. Let's learn to respect the silence of the scriptures and to speak where the Bible speaks.

~ 44 ~
Some Things God Is Not

Introduction

I.   There are many ideas held in regard to God.

II.   God is not what many people think He is.

Discussion

I.   God is not a respecter of persons.

    A. Romans 2:11

    B. Ephesians 6:9

    C. Acts 10:34-35

    D. If some are predestined to be lost or saved without their will, God would be a respecter of persons.

    E. Thus, God demands the same from all men.

II.   God is not a man.

    A. God is not human.

    B. Numbers 23:19

    C. 1 Samuel 15:29

    D. God is a spirit.

        1. John 4:24

      2. Luke 24:39

    E. Thus, God does not think as does a man (Isaiah 55:8-9).

III. God is not mocked.

    A. You might mock men but not God (Job 13:9).

    B. The word "mock" means to sneer at, deride, or to turn up your nose at.

    C. God has spoken His will, and God will not allow man to get out of reaping what he sows (Galatians 6:7).

      1. Hebrews 2:2

      2. God means what He says.

IV. God is not the cause of confusion.

    A. That confusion exists in the religious world, none would deny.

    B. Not God's fault

    C. 1 Corinthians 14:33

    D. God wants unity among His people.

      1. Psalms 133:1

      2. John 17:20-21

      3. 1 Corinthians 1:10

      4. Ephesians 4:1-6

    E. Man causes the division and the confusion.

V. God cannot be tempted with evil.

    A. James 1:12-15

    B. God is such that temptation in no way affects Him.

    C. Man tried to tempt divinity (Matthew 22:35).

    D. Satan tried it (Matthew 4:1-11).

      E. Yet, no sin.

VI.   God is not the God of the dead.

      A. Matthew 22:32

      B. Read and discuss the context (Matthew 22:23-32).

      C. Thus, God is not dead but alive!

VII.   God is not one to forget.

      A. Hebrews 6:10

      B. Some think that, as time passes, God will forget their sin. He will not.

      C. Some fail to work, thinking God will forget their labor.

          1. Hebrews 6:10

          2. 1 Corinthians 15:58

VIII. God is not ashamed to be called our God.

      A. Hebrews 11:16

      B. Romans 8:16-17

      C. Yet, some seem to be ashamed to be His children.

      D. Revelation 21:1-4

Conclusion

I.   Having learned some things God is not

      A. You will want to obey His will.

      B. Hear, believe, repent, confess and be baptized

II.   Come right now as we sing.

~ 45 ~
The People of God
Hebrews 8:7-10

Introduction

I.   God has always had those known as His people.

    A. Exodus 6:7

    B. Deuteronomy 4:20

    C. Jeremiah 13:11

    D. Luke 1:17

    E. Acts 15:14

    F. 1 Peter 2:9-10

II.   We need to know how the Bible describes His people.

    A. This can be used as a checklist.

    B. You will need to make personal application.

Discussion

I.   The people God are a few people.

    A. Deuteronomy 7:7

    B. Matthew 7:13-14

    C. Matthew 20:16

    D. Only these eight souls were saved in the days of Noah (1 Peter 3:20)

      E. Revelation 3:4

      F. God's people have always been in the minority!

      G. Yet many think the majority makes a thing right. Not so!

II.   The people of God are a peaceful people.

      A. God's people strive for peace, not war.

      B. Isaiah 32:17-18

      C. Here is a prophecy describing the peaceful nature of the church (Isaiah 2:2-4).

      D. Romans 14:17-19; Romans 12:18; 1 Timothy 2:1-2

III.   The people of God are a free people.

      A. Men are made free by the word of God (John 8:32; John 17:17).

      B. John 8:36

      C. Romans 6:17-18

      D. Romans 6:22

      E. Freedom must not be misused (Galatians 5:13; 1 Peter 2:16).

      F. Galatians 4:31

      G. Freedom is not license to do as one pleases.

            1. There are laws and regulations that must be respected.

            2. True in regard to hunting or driving a car

IV.   The people of God are an observing people.

      A. "Observe" means to keep, to adhere to; follow, pay attention to.

      B. God has always demanded that His people be observing.

    C. Matthew 28:18-20

    D. 1 Timothy 5:21

    E. There are some things not to be observed (Galatians 4:10).

V. The people of God are an abiding people.

    A. John 15:1-8

    B. 1 John 2:28

    C. Must abide in the doctrine of Christ (2 John 9-11)

    D. Must abide in the love of Christ (John 15:10)

    E. Must abide in the light (1 John 2:10; 1 John 1:7)

VI. The people of God are a submitting people.

    A. It is difficult to get some people to submit to God.

    B. "Submit" means to yield to the control of another.

    C. The church is to submit to Christ (Ephesians 5:24).

    D. We must submit to

        1. God (Hebrews 12:9)

        2. Gospel (2 Corinthians 9:13)

        3. God's righteousness (Romans 10:1-3)

        4. Powers that be (Romans 13:1-3)

        5. Children to parents (1 Timothy 3:4)

        6. Wives to husbands (Ephesians 5:22)

VII. The people of God are a ready people.

    A. John's work was to make a ready people (Luke 1:17).

    B. God's people must be ready

        1. To answer (1 Peter 3:15)

    2. To die (Acts 21:13; 2 Timothy 4:6-8)

    3. For the judgment (Matthew 25:10; Mark 13:32-37)

Conclusion

I.   Why not make yourself ready now by obeying the gospel and then work to be the people of God?

II.   Are you among the people of God?

~ 46 ~
The First Church
Matthew 16:13-19

Introduction

I.   Many are confused as to the first church.

    A. No need for the confusion

    B. The Bible is plain on the subject.

II. Read and discuss Matthew 16:13-19.

Discussion

I.   The first church was not

    A. A denomination—nothing about it was denominated

    B. The Catholic church—the Bible says nothing about the Catholic church

    C. A social club (Romans 14:17)

II. The first church was

    A. Established by Jesus Christ

        1. Matthew 16:18

        2. A warning (Psalms 127:1)

        3. The word is the seed. Just plant it and it produces the church (Luke 8:11).

    B. The church of Christ

        1. Romans 16:16

        2. Belongs to Christ

    C. One in number

        1. Ephesians 4:4

        2. Colossians 1:18

        3. 1 Corinthians 12:20

    D. The saved

        1. Acts 2:47

        2. Ephesians 5:23

III. Did not have

    A. Any reverends

        1. Matthew 23:8-9

        2. The word is only found one time in the Bible and then refers to God, not man (Psalms 111:9).

        3. Did you ever read of Rev. Peter, Rev. James and Rev. John? No! Just Peter, James and John.

    B. Instrumental music and worship

        1. Ephesians 5:19

        2. Colossians 3:16

        3. 1 Corinthians 14:15

        4. Hebrews 2:12

        5. The first church just sang.

    C. To depend upon any human organization for its existence

        1. The first church was complete and sufficient.

      2. Preached the word (1 Thessalonians 1:8)

      3. Took care of its own needy (Acts 6:1-6)

      4. Many today seem to think that the church could not exist without human institutions.

  D. A human creed book

      1. Just taught the word of God

      2. 2 Timothy 3:16-17

      3. 2 Peter 1:3

      4. Colossians 3:17

IV. Some things the first church had

  A. Christ as head

      1. Colossians 1:18

      2. Ephesians 1:22-23

  B. Elders in every church

      1. Acts 14:23

      2. Titus 1:5

  C. The Lord's supper weekly

      1. Acts 20:7

      2. Every week has a first day.

      3. I saw a sign that said, "The Lion's Club meets here Tuesday."

         a. How often did they meet?

         b. If you can see through a barrel with both ends knocked out, you can see this!

  D. One means of raising money

      1. 1 Corinthians 16:1-2

      2. No fund-raising campaigns devised by men

  E. Had problems

      1. People lying (Acts 5:1-11)

      2. Brethren going to law with one another (1 Corinthians 6)

      3. Fornicators (1 Corinthians 5)

      4. Marriage (1 Corinthians 7)

      5. Resurrection (1 Corinthians 15)

      6. Don't let problems get you down—work them out and go on!

V.   The first church had some things which we do not have.

  A. Spiritual gifts

      1. 1 Corinthians 12

      2. They served their purpose and have been done away with (1 Corinthians 13:8-10).

  B. Apostles

      1. Acts 1:22

      2. The qualifications of an apostle (seeing the Lord after His resurrection) shows that we do not have any today.

  C. Some customs

      1. Holy kiss (Romans 16:16)—we shake hands today

      2. Covering (1 Corinthians 11:4-16)

  D. Situations due to the present distress

      1. 1 Corinthians 7:26

      2. Paul was not opposed to marriage, but the times made it difficult on a married person.

E. Gospel in earthen vessels

   1. 2 Corinthians 4:7

   2. The first church had the gospel in the men—we have it in the book.

   3. Ephesians 4:3-5

Conclusion

I.   Would you like to be a member of the first church?

II.   Do what those people did to become a member, and you will be a member of the same church. Come now and obey as we sing.

~ 47 ~
Glad Words in the Bible

Introduction

I.   Some words in the Bible are sad words, but there are also glad words in the Bible.

II.   For encouragement, let us take a look at some glad words in the Bible.

Discussion

I.   "For He shall save his people from their sins"

    A. Man is a sinner and needs to be saved (Romans 3:23; 1 John 3:4)

    B. Jesus came to save man.

    C. Matthew 1:21

    D. Luke 19:10

    E. 1 Timothy 1:15

    F. Hebrews 2:9

    G. Hebrews 7:25

    H. Hebrews 5:8-9

    I. Revelation 1:5

II.   "For God so loved the world"

A. John 3:16

B. Romans 5:8

C. 1 Timothy 2:3-4

D. 2 Peter 3:9

E. Take John 3:16 and emphasize each word.

III. "I perceive that God is no respecter of persons"

A. Acts 10:34-35

B. Discuss context

C. Romans 2:11

D. I am glad that God is not a respecter of persons.

1. He could have made plans whereby only the educated, the rich or those of certain culture could be saved.

2. He did not, for He is not a respecter of persons.

IV. "There is made of necessity a change also of the law"

A. Hebrews 7:12

B. These are glad words that the law has been changed.

1. The old law made nothing perfect (Hebrews 7:19).

2. Could not take away sin (Hebrews 10:1-4; 11)

3. Was a yoke of bondage (Galatians 5:1; Galatians 4:25)

C. A change in the law made possible the new law of Christ.

1. Galatians 6:2

2. We can be married to Christ (Romans 7:4).

3. We can have our sins forgiven and forgotten (Hebrews 10:17).

V. "Whereby when ye read, ye may understand"

   A. Ephesians 3:4

   B. Study context (Ephesians 3:1-5)

   C. I myself, can read and understand the word of God.

   D. These are glad words, for

      1. My faith does not have to stand in the wisdom of men (1 Corinthians 2:5).

      2. I can search the Scriptures to see if things are so (Acts 17:11; John 5:39).

      3. I can work out my own salvation (Philippians 2:12).

      4. I can study the book I will be judged by (John 12:48; Romans 2:16).

VI. "Heirs of God and joint heirs with Christ"

   A. Romans 8:17

   B. Conditional: "if children"

   C. Discuss being a child of God.

      1. Seed (Luke 8:11; 1 Peter 1:23)

      2. Born again (John 3:3-5)

      3. A child of God's family (Ephesians 3:15)

      4. Must be faithful (1 Corinthians 15:58)

   D. The future blessings of God's people are in the form of an inheritance.

      1. Matthew 25:34

      2. Acts 20:32

      3. Hebrews 6:12

      4. 1 Peter 1:3-4

Conclusion

I.   Have you taken advantage of these glad words in the Bible?

II.   You can, right now, as we sing. Come believing and obeying.

~ 48 ~
Some Things Christ Does Not Know

Introduction

I.   It is not the purpose of this sermon to limit the power or knowledge of Christ.

    A. Knew who would betray Him (John 13:11)

    B. Knows man (John 2:25)

    C. Knows man's thoughts (Matthew 12:25)

II.   Yet there are some things we can learn from this theme.

Discussion

I.   First, Christ knew no sin.

    A. 2 Corinthians 5:21

    B. Hebrews 4:15

    C. 1 Peter 1:21-24

    D. Example of Jesus being tempted, yet no sin (Matthew 4:1-11)

    E. Hebrews 7:25-28

    F. Jesus, though human as well as divine, never did commit one sin!

II.   Christ does not know when He will return the second time.

A. Many have set the time for the second coming of Christ.

B. Christ Himself does not know.

    1. Matthew 13:32-37

    2. Only God the Father knows, and he has not told anyone (Matthew 24:36)!

C. There are no signs of His second coming.

    1. Matthew 24 deals with the destruction of Jerusalem, which occurred in 70 A.D.

    2. Matthew 24:34

III. Christ does not know a person he did not die for.

A. Jesus tasted death for every man.

    1. Hebrews 2:9

    2. Not a pre-selected few

    3. 1 Corinthians 15:3

    4. Romans 5:15-19

B. Man must obey.

    1. Hebrews 5:8-9

    2. Luke 6:46

IV. If Christ is coming back to earth to set up an earthly kingdom, Christ does not know it.

A. The kingdom has been set up (Matthew 16:18-19; Hebrews 12:23; Colossians 1:13).

B. Christ is reigning now (Acts 2:32-36).

C. Kingdom will be delivered back to God when He comes (1 Corinthians 15:23-24).

V. Christ knows of no other name by which men can be saved than by His.

    A. He has an exalted name (Philippians 2:9-11)

    B. Salvation in no other name (Acts 4:11-12)

VI. Knows nothing about establishing any church but His own

    A. Psalms 127:1

    B. Matthew 16:18

    C. Romans 16:16

    D. Acts 2:47

    E. Acts 20:28

    F. The New Testament only reveals the Lord's church.

VII. Knows of no person who can come to the Father except by Him

    A. He is the way to the Father (John 14:1-6).

    B. Must be taught (John 6:44-45)

    C. Called by the gospel (2 Thessalonians 2:14)

    D. He is the door (John 10:9-10).

    E. He is the mediator (1 Timothy 2:5).

VIII. Knows of no head of the church but Himself

    A. Ephesians 1:22-23

    B. Colossians 1:18

    C. Ephesians 5:23-24

    D. Human churches have human heads.

    E. The Lord's church has a divine head.

Conclusion

I. Christ knows nothing about any plan of salvation but the one taught in the New Testament.

II. Come right now by hearing, believing, repenting, confessing and being baptized.

~ 49 ~
When the Day of Pentecost Was Come

Introduction

I. Pentecost was a feast day of Old Testament Jews. It was a Jewish harvest-home. Pentecost means fifty, in that it occurred fifty days after the Passover (Leviticus 23:15-16). The word is found three times in the Bible (Acts 2:1; 20:16; 1 Corinthians 16:8), but is never mentioned by name in the Old Testament. It was one of the three annual feasts of the Israelites (Exodus 34:22; Deuteronomy 16:16) called the feast of weeks.

II. Pentecost was not a church, but a day (Acts 2:1).

III. This lesson takes a look at some events which took place "when the day of Pentecost was come."

Discussion

I. The apostles were found in Jerusalem.

   A. Luke 2:46-49; Acts 1:4-8; Acts 2:1

   B. They were ordered there by the Lord.

II. There was tongue speaking.

   A. Acts 2:2-3; Acts 2:6-11

   B. The apostles spoke in the languages of the people present (Acts 2:6, 11).

      C. Tongue speaking was one of the spiritual gifts bestowed by the laying on of an apostle's hand (1 Corinthians 12:1-10; Acts 8:14-18; Acts 19:1-6).

III.   The Holy Spirit was received by the apostles.

      A. The Holy Spirit was promised to the apostles (John 14:26; John 16:13).

      B. The Holy Spirit was received by the apostles (Acts 1:2; Acts 2:1-4). This was the baptism of the Holy Spirit, promised by the Lord (Matthew 3:11).

IV.   Old Testament prophecy was fulfilled.

      A. Acts 2:12-17

      B. Joel 2:28-29

      C. 2 Peter 1:19-21

V.   Gospel preaching began.

      A. The great commission is being carried out, as given to the apostles (Matthew 28:19; Mark 16:15-16; Luke 24:46-49; Acts 1:8).

      B. The first gospel sermon is preached by all the apostles; Peter's is recorded (Acts 2:22-36).

VI.   The plan of salvation was taught.

      A. Acts 2:37-38; Acts 2:41

      B. Men heard, believed, repented and were baptized.

VII.   The church of Christ began.

      A. The prophecy of Isaiah 2:2-3 is being fulfilled.

      B. Acts 2:5; Acts 2:16-17

      C. Acts 2:47

      D. The church of Christ has begun (Romans 16:16).

Conclusion

I.   These early Christians "continued" (Acts 2:42; Hebrews 2:12).

II. You need to do the same as these did on Pentecost.

III. Come just now as we sing.

~ 50 ~
When the Church Grew

Introduction

I.   We all must be interested in the church growing.

II.   As individuals, we are taught to grow.

     A. 1 Peter 2:2

     B. 2 Peter 3:18

III.   This sermon looks at when the church grew in New Testament times.

Discussion

I.   When the seed was put in the soil

     A. There will not be much of a 'crop' of converts if the "seed is yet in the barn" (Haggai 2:19).

     B. The seed is the word of God (Luke 8:11).

     C. In New Testament days, the church grew when the seed was planted in the soil, or the hearts of men and women (Luke 8:5-15).

     D. Examples of this seed-planting can be seen in the conversions of Acts 2-19.

II.   When discipline was practiced

A. When Ananias and Sapphira were disciplined with physical death for lying, the church grew (Acts 5:1-11).

B. Notice how "the believers were the more added to the Lord, multitudes both of men and women" (Acts 5:14) when there was discipline.

C. If we expect the church to grow today, discipline must be exercised when needed (1 Corinthians 5; 2 Thessalonians 3:6-15).

III. When the church did its own work

A. Acts 6:1-6 finds the church taking care of its own widows.

B. As a result of this work, "word of God increased; and the number of the disciples multiplied in Jerusalem greatly; and a great company of the priests were obedient to the faith" (Acts 6:7).

C. The local church is all-sufficient to do its own work today (1 Timothy 3:15).

IV. When the church was at rest or peace

A. Who wants to be part of a fussing, fighting church?

B. Some today "bite and devour one another" (Galatians 5:15).

C. Acts 9:31 finds the church at rest.

D. When the church had rest and peace, growth came to this church as they "multiplied" (Acts 9:31)!

V. When the church burned some bad books

A. Acts 19:19

B. Are there any bad books being read in your home?

C. Do you know what your young people are seeing and reading? You better!

D. Notice the effect of getting rid of this filth (Acts 19:20). It will still work.

VI. When the church keeps God's decrees

A. To keep God's decrees is to obey His doctrine as expressed by His authority.

B. Acts 16:4

C. Now notice how this brought about daily church growth (Acts 16:5).

Conclusion

I. If these things brought about church growth in the first century, they will in our century.

II. Let's get to work and get the job done, now!

www.ingramcontent.com/pod-product-compliance
Lightning Source LLC
Chambersburg PA
CBHW070331090426
42733CB00012B/2435